Exploring The Afterlife Theory

Exploring The Afterlife Theory

Doug Hensley

CONTENTS

**"Beyond the Veil:
Journeys in the Afterlife"
By
Doug Hensley**

Chapter 18: The Reincarnation

Author's Notes

"In a realm beyond life as we know it, Sarah embarks on an extraordinary journey through the afterlife. From the mysterious Temple of Reflection to the ethereal Symphony of Souls, she explores realms of wisdom, unity, and love that challenge the very fabric of existence. As Sarah's quest unfolds, she discovers that the key to her own transformation lies not in knowledge alone, but in the boundless power of love and compassion. Join her on this riveting odyssey of the soul, where the mysteries of the afterlife come alive, and the heart reveals the true essence of existence."

Chapter 1: The Protagonist's Death

The night was cold and drizzling, a fitting backdrop to the tragic events that were about to unfold. Sarah, our protagonist, had never paid much attention to the weather, but that night, it seemed like even the heavens were mourning. She was driving along a winding road, her hands gripping the steering wheel with white-knuckled intensity. Her heart raced, not just from the rain-slicked roads, but from the argument she'd had with her best friend, Mark, just moments ago.

The argument had been explosive, a culmination of months of tension and misunderstandings. Sarah had wanted to make amends, to set things right between them, but Mark had been adamant, his anger unyielding. He had slammed the door of their shared apartment, leaving Sarah in a cloud of frustration and hurt.

As the headlights of her car cut through the darkness, Sarah's thoughts were in turmoil. She wished she could turn back time, erase the bitter words exchanged between them, and tell Mark how much he meant to her. But it was too late for that now.

Her phone buzzed, a message notification that she instinctively reached for. It was a text from Mark, a simple "I'm sorry" followed by a heart emoji. Tears blurred her vision as she read it. She was about to reply when the sound of screeching tires and blaring horns shattered the night.

Sarah's car swerved out of control, a sickening sensation of weightlessness engulfing her as it veered off the road. Time seemed to slow as her car tumbled down an embankment, the world spinning in a dizzying whirl of lights and sounds. She caught glimpses of trees, rain-slicked leaves, and the dark expanse of the night sky.

Then, there was a deafening crash, and everything went black.

When Sarah regained consciousness, it wasn't the blinding white light she had heard about in stories of near-death experiences. Instead, she found herself in a place that felt strangely familiar, yet entirely different. It was as if she had stepped into a dreamscape, a world of ethereal beauty.

She was standing in a meadow bathed in a soft, silvery light. The grass beneath her feet was impossibly lush and vibrant, and the air carried a scent of blooming flowers and earthy freshness. The sky above was a mesmerizing blend of colors that shifted and changed like a living canvas. It was a place of breathtaking beauty, unlike anything she had ever seen.

Confusion gripped Sarah. She touched her body, half-expecting to find herself injured or in pain, but she felt nothing. She was whole, unharmed, and wearing the same clothes she had on before the accident.

"Where am I?" she whispered to herself, her voice barely more than a breath of wind.

As if in answer to her question, a figure began to materialize before her. It was a woman, radiant and graceful, with eyes that seemed to hold the wisdom of ages. She wore a flowing gown that shimmered like liquid silver, and her presence exuded a sense of profound serenity.

"Welcome, Sarah," the woman said, her voice a melodic blend of warmth and reassurance. "You have crossed over to the other side, to the realm beyond life as you know it."

Sarah's heart raced as she tried to make sense of it all. "Am I... am I dead?"

The woman nodded gently. "Yes, but fear not, for this is not the end. It is a new beginning."

Tears welled up in Sarah's eyes as the weight of her own mortality settled upon her. She had so many questions, so many uncertainties about what lay ahead. But one thing was clear: her journey in the afterlife had just begun.

And so, in that surreal meadow bathed in silver light, Sarah took her first step into the unknown, leaving behind the world she knew for a realm where the mysteries of life and death would unfold in ways she could never have imagined.

This extended version of Chapter 1 sets the stage for Sarah's journey in the afterlife and introduces the mysterious woman who will guide her. You can continue to develop the story, exploring Sarah's emotions, her interactions in this new realm, and the mysteries that lie ahead in subsequent chapters.

Chapter 2: Awakening in the Afterlife

Sarah stood in the meadow, her eyes fixed on the enigmatic woman who had welcomed her to this otherworldly realm. The woman's presence exuded a sense of peace and understanding that washed over Sarah like a soothing balm.

"I know this is overwhelming," the woman said, her voice a comforting melody. "But you are safe here, Sarah."

Sarah nodded, her thoughts a whirlwind of confusion and wonder. She took in her surroundings once more, noticing the subtle details that made this place unlike anything she had ever experienced. The grass beneath her feet seemed to emit a soft, melodic hum, as if it were alive. Flowers of every hue danced in the gentle breeze, their petals emitting a gentle glow.

As she continued to survey her surroundings, Sarah realized that there were others in the meadow with her. Souls, like herself, who had crossed over from the world of the living. Some were sitting in small groups, engaged in hushed conversations, while others wandered alone, lost in thought.

The woman gestured toward the souls in the meadow. "These are your fellow travelers, Sarah. Souls from all walks of life, each with their own unique journey."

Sarah watched in awe as the souls moved about, their forms radiant and translucent, like faintly glowing stars. She couldn't help but wonder about the stories hidden within each one, the experiences that had led them to this place.

The woman extended a hand toward Sarah. "Come, let me show you more of this realm."

With a sense of curiosity and a trace of trepidation, Sarah took the woman's hand. They began to walk through the meadow, and as they did, Sarah noticed that the silvery light surrounding them seemed to respond to their presence, creating intricate patterns in the air.

"What is this place?" Sarah finally managed to ask.

The woman smiled gently. "This is a place of transition, a realm between the world of the living and what lies beyond. Some call it the Threshold. Here, souls like yours find solace, healing, and guidance before continuing their journey."

Sarah absorbed the words, trying to make sense of her new reality. "But what happens next? Where do we go from here?"

The woman's eyes held a hint of mystery. "That, my dear, depends on the choices you make, the lessons you learn, and the path you follow. The afterlife is vast and full of possibilities."

As they walked, they came upon a tranquil pond, its surface as smooth as glass. Sarah could see her reflection, but it was not the reflection of the person she had been in life. It was a reflection of her true essence, her soul, free from the constraints of her earthly form.

"Who am I now?" Sarah whispered, her voice trembling.

The woman's gaze remained fixed on the pond. "You are who you have always been, Sarah. You are a soul, a being of light and energy, bound by neither time nor space. In this realm, you are your truest self."

Sarah felt a mixture of awe and acceptance wash over her. She had spent her life searching for meaning, for a sense of purpose. Now, in this otherworldly place, she had the opportunity to discover who she truly was.

As they continued their journey, Sarah couldn't help but

think of the world she had left behind—the people she loved, the dreams she had pursued, and the mistakes she had made. It was a bittersweet reflection, a reminder of the complexity of her human existence.

The woman turned to her, her eyes filled with compassion. "You carry the memories of your earthly life with you, Sarah. They are a part of your journey, a part of what makes you who you are."

Tears welled up in Sarah's eyes as she thought of the people she had lost, the moments of joy and sorrow that had shaped her. She wasn't sure what lay ahead in this afterlife, but one thing was certain: it was a place of profound transformation and discovery.

And so, in that tranquil meadow, surrounded by the radiant souls of fellow travelers, Sarah began to embrace the mysteries of the afterlife, ready to embark on a journey that would challenge her, heal her, and ultimately lead her to the answers she sought.

Chapter 3: The Welcome Committee

As Sarah walked alongside the radiant woman through the tranquil meadow, she couldn't help but feel a sense of peace and wonder settling within her. The meadow stretched on, seemingly endless, but each step she took was a step further into the mysteries of the afterlife.

As they walked, the woman began to explain more about this realm. "Many souls arrive here in various states of confusion and uncertainty. That's where we come in, those of us who have been here for some time. We help newcomers like you acclimate to this new existence."

Sarah nodded, grateful for the guidance. "How long have you been here?"

The woman's smile held a touch of ancient wisdom. "Time is different in this place, Sarah. It's not measured as it is in the world of the living. I've been here for what you might perceive as a long time, but it feels both eternal and fleeting."

As they continued to walk, Sarah noticed figures approaching in the distance. They were other beings like the woman, their forms shimmering with a gentle radiance. They gathered around, forming a welcoming committee of sorts. Each one had a unique presence, and their eyes held a depth of understanding that seemed to reach into the very essence of Sarah's being.

One of the beings, a man with a serene countenance, stepped forward. "Welcome, Sarah. I am Elias. We are here to assist you on your journey through the afterlife."

Sarah extended her hand to shake his, but to her surprise, their hands passed through each other as if they were made of mist. She withdrew her hand, momentarily taken aback.

Elias chuckled warmly. "In this realm, physical touch is not necessary. We communicate on a different level, one that transcends the limitations of the physical world."

Sarah nodded, still trying to grasp the nature of this existence. "I have so many questions. What is this place, and what comes next?"

Elias gestured toward the meadow and the souls who moved about. "This is a place of transition, a realm where souls find healing, reflection, and guidance. What comes next is a journey unique to each soul. Some choose to move on to higher realms, while others may opt for reincarnation."

Sarah's mind buzzed with curiosity. "Reincarnation? You mean I could come back to life?"

Elias nodded. "Yes, if you choose to do so. Reincarnation is an opportunity for further growth and learning. It allows your soul to experience different aspects of existence."

The thought of returning to the world of the living filled Sarah with a mix of excitement and trepidation. She had so many unresolved questions, unfulfilled dreams, and relationships she wished she could mend. The idea of a second chance was tantalizing.

Another being, a woman with luminous eyes, stepped forward. "But that decision is not one to be made hastily, Sarah. Your experiences in this realm will help you understand the implications of your choices."

Sarah nodded, realizing that she had much to learn about the afterlife and herself. She looked around at the welcoming committee, a group of souls who had undoubtedly faced their own trials and tribulations in their journeys.

"What should I do now?" she asked.

Elias spoke with a gentle tone. "First, take your time to explore this place, to reflect on your life, and to seek understanding. You'll have opportunities to revisit your memories and learn from your experiences. We'll be here to guide you every step of the way."

And so, Sarah embarked on her journey in the afterlife, surrounded by the radiant beings of the welcome committee and the enigmatic woman who had greeted her. The meadow was just the beginning, a place of healing and transformation where her true exploration of the afterlife would unfold.

In this extended Chapter 3, Sarah encounters the welcoming committee of beings who help newcomers like her adjust to the afterlife. They provide her with information about the nature of this realm and the choices that lie ahead. Sarah's journey of self-discovery and understanding begins to take shape, and she realizes that the afterlife holds many secrets and opportunities for growth.

Chapter 4: Revisiting Life Memories

In the days that followed her arrival in the afterlife, Sarah found herself drawn to a unique place within the ethereal realm—an expansive garden where the boundaries of time and memory seemed to blur. This garden held the key to one of the most profound experiences in the afterlife—the opportunity to revisit the memories of her life.

Guided by the luminous beings who had welcomed her, Sarah entered the garden. The air was filled with the scent of blossoms, and the soft music of nature's orchestra played in the background, creating an atmosphere of serenity. The path she walked upon was paved with iridescent stones that seemed to respond to her presence, illuminating her way.

The first memory that came to her was of her childhood home. As she stepped onto a cobblestone pathway, the scene around her transformed. She found herself standing in front of the familiar house where she had spent her early years. The sound of children's laughter filled the air, and she saw her younger self playing in the front yard.

Tears welled up in her eyes as she watched herself, a

carefree child with dreams and innocence. She could feel the warmth of her mother's embrace and the reassuring presence of her father. It was a time of wonder and simplicity, a time when life's complexities had not yet cast their shadow.

The luminous beings who accompanied her watched with understanding. Elias spoke softly, "These memories hold the essence of who you are, Sarah. They are the threads that weave the tapestry of your soul."

As the scene shifted to her teenage years, Sarah saw herself again, filled with the hopes and dreams of adolescence. She remembered the joy of her first crush, the thrill of late-night conversations with friends, and the taste of freedom as she ventured into the world on her own.

But there were also moments of pain and heartache, like the memory of a broken friendship that had haunted her for years. She had always wished she could go back and make amends, and now, in this place, she felt the weight of those unspoken apologies.

The luminous woman who had first greeted her placed a hand on her shoulder. "You have the power to heal old wounds here, to understand the choices you made and the impact they had on others."

Sarah nodded, realizing that this garden of memories was not just a place of reflection but also a place of healing and growth. She watched as the scenes of her life continued to unfold, from the highs of love and achievement to the lows of loss and disappointment.

One memory, in particular, stood out—the day she had stood up to defend a classmate who was being bullied. It was a moment of courage she had almost forgotten, buried beneath the weight of other memories. She saw the grateful smile on her classmate's face, a smile that held the promise of friendship and acceptance.

Elias spoke again, his voice gentle. "These memories are the building blocks of your soul's evolution, Sarah. They are the lessons that shape your path in the afterlife."

As Sarah continued to explore her life's memories, she began to understand the intricate tapestry of her existence. Each moment, whether joyful or painful, had played a role in shaping the person she had become. She realized that her journey in the afterlife was not just about moving forward but also about reconciling with her past.

In the garden of memories, Sarah found solace and clarity. She revisited the moments of love, forgiveness, and growth, and she acknowledged the moments of pain, regret, and missed opportunities. It was a profound journey of self-discovery, a journey that would prepare her for the choices and challenges that lay ahead in the afterlife.

And so, as the memories of her life continued to unfold in the garden, Sarah embraced the lessons they held, knowing that they were the threads that would guide her on her path of transformation in the afterlife.

This extended Chapter 4 delves deeper into Sarah's exploration of her life's memories and the profound lessons they hold. It highlights the healing and growth that can occur in the afterlife as she comes to terms with the complexities of her past. The garden of memories becomes a pivotal setting for her journey of self-discovery.

Chapter 5: The Soul's Journey

In the days that followed Sarah's exploration of the garden of memories, she found herself drawn to another aspect of the afterlife—a realm where souls embarked on journeys of self-discovery and transformation. This realm was a place of exploration and growth, where each soul had the opportunity to understand the depths of their being.

Guided by Elias, the serene being who had become her mentor of sorts, Sarah entered the realm of the soul's journey. It was a vast and ever-changing landscape, filled with landscapes that defied earthly description. Mountains of crystal and rivers of liquid light stretched out before her.

Elias gestured to the breathtaking panorama. "This is where you'll come to understand the nature of your soul, Sarah. Here, you'll embark on a journey of self-discovery and exploration."

Sarah felt a mixture of awe and anticipation as she took in her surroundings. The air was charged with an energy that seemed to pulse with life. She could sense the presence of other souls moving about, each on their unique journeys of understanding.

Her first destination was a crystalline mountain that beckoned to her with an irresistible allure. As she climbed its radiant slopes, she felt a sense of exhilaration and clarity wash over her. The mountain was not just a physical place but a reflection of her inner self, a representation of her aspirations and dreams.

At the summit, Sarah was met by the luminous woman who had first welcomed her to the afterlife. "This mountain is a mirror of your soul's highest aspirations, Sarah. What do you see?"

Sarah gazed out at the breathtaking vista below, a panorama that seemed to stretch on forever. She saw images of the dreams she had once held—the desire to create art, the longing for deep connections, and the quest for knowledge. But she also saw the dreams she had yet to fulfill, the potential waiting to be unlocked.

With newfound clarity, she understood that her journey in the afterlife was not just about reflecting on the past but also about envisioning the future. She felt a renewed sense of purpose, a commitment to pursue her soul's deepest desires.

Elias appeared beside her, his presence a source of guidance and support. "Your journey is a continuous cycle of growth, Sarah. Each step leads to greater self-awareness and understanding."

The next destination on her journey led her to a river of liquid light, where she witnessed scenes from her life replayed in shimmering patterns on the water's surface. It was a river of reflection, a place where she could gain insights into the choices she had made and their impact on her journey.

She watched moments of kindness and compassion, moments of strength and resilience. But she also witnessed moments of doubt and hesitation, moments when fear had held her back. It was a sobering experience, a reminder of the complexities of her humanity.

As she continued her journey, Sarah encountered other souls who shared their stories and insights. She learned about the diverse paths and experiences that had brought them to this realm. Each encounter was a reminder of the interconnectedness of all souls, a web of experiences and lessons that spanned across time and space.

One particularly profound encounter was with a soul who had chosen the path of forgiveness and reconciliation. This soul had experienced great pain and betrayal in life but had found the strength to forgive and heal. The encounter left Sarah with a deep sense of inspiration and the realization that forgiveness was a powerful force that could transform not only individuals but also the world.

As days turned into weeks in the realm of the soul's journey, Sarah's understanding of herself and the afterlife deepened. She began to see her journey not as a linear progression but as a series of interconnected experiences and lessons. Each step was a building block in her soul's evolution, a step closer to realizing her true potential.

And so, in the ever-changing landscape of the afterlife, Sarah embraced the soul's journey with open arms. She knew that the path ahead was filled with challenges and revelations, but she was determined to explore the depths of her being and discover the true essence of her soul.

This extended Chapter 5 delves deeper into Sarah's exploration of the afterlife, specifically the realm of the soul's journey. It explores the transformative experiences and encounters she has along the way and highlights the interconnectedness of souls in this realm. Sarah's journey of self-discovery and growth continues to unfold, shaping her understanding of the afterlife and her place within it.

Chapter 6: Meeting Lost Loved Ones

In the luminous world of the afterlife, Sarah's journey of self-discovery continued to unfold, revealing new facets of her existence with each passing day. Yet, among the countless revelations and encounters, one held a unique place in her heart—the opportunity to reunite with her lost loved ones.

Guided by Elias, the serene being who had become her mentor and guide, Sarah embarked on a journey to reconnect with those who had passed on before her. The thought of seeing her departed family and friends filled her with a mixture of anticipation and emotion. She wondered if they had found peace and happiness in this ethereal realm.

As they walked together through a radiant forest, Elias spoke softly, "The bonds of love and connection are not broken by death, Sarah. They continue to exist in this realm, where the essence of each soul endures."

Sarah's heart swelled with hope as they approached a clearing within the forest. There, in a soft and golden light, she saw familiar faces waiting for her. Her parents, her grandparents, and friends who had departed before her stood with open arms, their smiles radiant with love.

Tears of joy streamed down Sarah's cheeks as she rushed toward them. The sense of reunion was overwhelming as she embraced her parents, feeling the warmth and love that transcended the boundaries of earthly existence.

Her mother, her voice filled with love, spoke softly, "Welcome, dear. We've been waiting for you."

Sarah looked around at the familiar faces, each person representing a cherished memory from her life. Her grandfather, who had taught her the joy of storytelling, shared a tale of an ancient adventure, and her childhood friend reminisced about their adventures in a secret hideaway.

As the hours passed, Sarah laughed and cried, shared stories and memories, and felt the profound sense of belonging that had eluded her in the world of the living. The barriers of time and distance dissolved, and she realized that this realm allowed for a depth of connection that was beyond her wildest dreams.

Her father, with a twinkle in his eye, said, "We've been watching over you, Sarah. We've seen your struggles and your triumphs. We've shared your joys and sorrows."

The realization that her loved ones had been with her, even in her darkest moments, brought a sense of comfort and reassurance. She felt their unconditional love and support in a way she had never imagined possible.

Elias, who had watched the reunion with a serene smile, approached her. "The bonds you share with your loved ones are eternal, Sarah. They are a source of strength and guidance on your journey in the afterlife."

Over the following days, Sarah continued to spend time with her departed loved ones, relishing the moments of connection and shared experiences. Together, they explored the luminous landscapes of the afterlife, embarking on adventures and discoveries that deepened their bonds.

One day, as they walked along the shores of a radiant lake, her grandmother, whose wisdom had always been a source of guidance, shared profound insights about the nature of existence. She spoke of the interconnectedness of all souls, the threads of energy that bound them together, and the endless possibilities of growth and transformation.

Sarah listened with rapt attention, realizing that her journey in the afterlife was not just about personal growth but also about contributing to the collective wisdom and evolution of all souls. The knowledge she gained from her loved ones and her own experiences would become a part of this greater tapestry of understanding.

As time flowed differently in the afterlife, Sarah cherished each moment with her loved ones, knowing that their reunion was not bound by the constraints of earthly time. She understood that this realm offered her the chance to deepen her connections, heal old wounds, and continue to learn from the wisdom of those who had gone before her.

And so, in the luminous world of the afterlife, Sarah's journey took on new dimensions as she reveled in the joy of reuniting with her lost loved ones. The bonds of love and connection that had transcended death became a source of strength and inspiration, guiding her on her path of self-discovery and growth.

This extended Chapter 6 delves deeper into Sarah's emotional reunion with her lost loved ones in the afterlife, highlighting the enduring nature of their connections and the wisdom they share. It explores the transformative impact of these reunions on Sarah's understanding of herself and her place in this ethereal realm.

Chapter 7: The Library of Life

As Sarah's journey through the afterlife continued, she discovered that this ethereal realm held more wonders than she could have ever imagined. One of the most remarkable places she encountered was the Library of Life—a place where the stories and experiences of every soul in existence were recorded.

Guided by Elias, her trusted mentor and companion, Sarah entered the library with a sense of reverence. The moment she stepped through its shimmering doors, she was enveloped in an atmosphere of wisdom and knowledge. The library stretched out endlessly in all directions, with towering shelves filled with bound volumes, each emanating a soft, radiant light.

Elias spoke, his voice filled with awe, "This is the repository of all existence, Sarah. Every soul's journey, every thought, every emotion, is recorded here."

Sarah's eyes widened in wonder as she gazed at the vastness of the library. "But how can everything be contained in this place?"

Elias smiled, a knowing glint in his eyes. "In the afterlife, space and time are not bound by the same limitations as in the world of the living. Here, the library exists as a reflection of the collective consciousness of all souls."

As they ventured deeper into the library, Sarah began to notice the bound volumes taking on a life of their own. They pulsed with energy, and as she reached out to touch one, she found herself immersed in a vivid and immersive experience—a glimpse into the life and experiences of a soul.

She watched a mother's loving embrace as she held her newborn child for the first time, felt the heartache of a soldier bidding farewell to his family before going off to war, and witnessed the exhilaration of an artist creating a masterpiece. Each volume held a unique story, a perspective on life that was both familiar and utterly unique.

One volume caught her attention—a simple leather-bound book that seemed to radiate a gentle warmth. She picked it up, and as she opened it, she found herself transported into her own life's story. She watched her childhood unfold, her dreams and aspirations taking shape, and the moments of triumph and tribulation that had shaped her journey.

Elias watched as Sarah delved into her own story, his expression filled with understanding. "The library not only contains the stories of others but also offers you the opportunity to gain insights into your own journey, to see the tapestry of your existence in its entirety."

Sarah nodded, her heart filled with a profound sense of gratitude. She saw the choices she had made, the paths she had taken, and the moments that had defined her. It was a journey of self-discovery, a chance to understand the significance of her own experiences.

As she continued to explore the library, Sarah encountered other souls who were also navigating the vast repository of knowledge. Some were seeking answers to profound questions, while others were reliving cherished memories or revisiting moments of regret.

One soul, a philosopher who had pondered the mysteries of existence in life, engaged Sarah in a deep conversation about the nature of consciousness and the interconnectedness of all souls. They explored the profound wisdom contained within the library and the idea that every soul's journey contributed to the collective evolution of consciousness.

Elias joined the conversation, adding his insights and guidance. "The library is a place of reflection and illumination, Sarah. It offers you the chance to gain a deeper understanding of the complexities of existence and your role in the grand tapestry of life."

As days turned into weeks within the Library of Life, Sarah's appreciation for the boundless knowledge it contained grew. She realized that this place was not just a repository of stories but also a source of profound wisdom, a reflection of the infinite possibilities of existence.

One day, as she stood before a particularly radiant volume, Elias spoke softly, "The library also holds the stories of those who have yet to be born, the souls waiting to embark on their own journeys. It is a reminder that life is a continuum, a cycle of growth and evolution."

Sarah nodded, her heart filled with a sense of purpose. She understood that her journey in the afterlife was not just about reflecting on the past but also about contributing to the future. The stories she would share, the wisdom she would gain, would become a part of the ever-expanding tapestry of existence.

And so, in the Library of Life, surrounded by the stories and experiences of countless souls, Sarah continued her journey of self-discovery and growth. She explored the mysteries of existence, gained profound insights into the nature of consciousness, and marveled at the boundless possibilities of life.

This extended Chapter 7 delves deeper into Sarah's

exploration of the afterlife, specifically her experience within the Library of Life. It highlights the profound wisdom and insights she gains from this remarkable place, as well as the opportunity to reflect on her own life's journey. The library becomes a symbol of the interconnectedness of all souls and the collective evolution of consciousness.

Chapter 8: The Trial of Self-Reflection

In the luminous world of the afterlife, Sarah's journey of self-discovery and growth continued to lead her to new and profound experiences. One of the most transformative challenges she encountered was the Trial of Self-Reflection—a test of her understanding, empathy, and ability to confront her own inner demons.

Guided by Elias, her trusted mentor, Sarah arrived at a place within the ethereal realm that seemed to shimmer with an otherworldly intensity. It was a place of introspection and revelation, where the boundaries of her own consciousness would be pushed to their limits.

Elias spoke with solemnity, "The Trial of Self-Reflection is a pivotal moment in your journey, Sarah. It will test your understanding of yourself and your capacity for empathy."

Sarah nodded, her heart filled with a mix of anticipation and trepidation. She knew that this trial would challenge her in ways she could not fully comprehend. She took a deep breath and entered the radiant chamber before her.

Inside, she found herself standing before a mirror—an immense, shimmering mirror that seemed to reflect not only her physical form but also the depths of her soul. As she gazed into it, she saw not just her own image but also the images of those she had encountered in her life—the people she had loved, the people she had hurt, and the people she had misunderstood.

Elias stood beside her, his presence a source of comfort and guidance. "The mirror reveals not only your own reflection, Sarah, but also the reflections of the souls you have touched in your journey."

Sarah's heart pounded as she watched the scenes in the mirror unfold. She saw moments of kindness and compassion, moments when she had offered a helping hand or a comforting word. Those images filled her with a sense of pride and warmth.

But there were also moments of pain and regret, moments when her actions had caused harm or when she had failed to understand the struggles of others. The mirror showed her the faces of people she had hurt, the wounds she had inflicted, and the words she wished she could take back.

Tears welled up in Sarah's eyes as she confronted the mistakes and shortcomings of her earthly existence. She saw the hurt in the eyes of a friend she had let down, the disappointment in a family member she had misunderstood, and the pain of a stranger she had ignored.

Elias spoke softly, his voice filled with compassion, "The Trial of Self-Reflection asks you to confront the shadows within yourself, Sarah. It is an opportunity to acknowledge your mistakes, seek forgiveness, and grow from your experiences."

Sarah nodded, her determination to face her own shortcomings unwavering. She knew that this trial was not about self-condemnation but about self-awareness and growth. She watched as the mirror continued to reveal moments from her life, both the moments of light and the moments of darkness.

As she gazed into the mirror, Sarah saw something unexpected—a reflection of herself as a child, innocent and full of wonder. It was a reminder of the pure and unblemished soul that she had once been, the essence of her true self.

With newfound clarity, she understood that the Trial of Self-Reflection was not just about acknowledging her mistakes but also about reclaiming her own innocence and authenticity. It was about reconnecting with the childlike wonder and compassion that had always resided within her.

As the trial continued, Sarah encountered the reflections of people from her past, including those she had lost touch with and those she had longed to reconnect with. The mirror became a portal to moments of forgiveness and reconciliation, as well as an opportunity to express remorse and seek forgiveness.

One reflection, in particular, stood out—a friend she had drifted apart from due to misunderstandings and miscommunications. Sarah watched as the mirror revealed a heartfelt conversation in which they both acknowledged their mistakes and rekindled their friendship. It was a moment of healing and renewal, a reminder that it was never too late to mend broken bonds.

Elias watched with a knowing smile. "The Trial of Self-Reflection is not just a test, Sarah, but also a chance for redemption and growth. It allows you to heal old wounds and forge deeper connections with the souls you have encountered."

As the trial reached its conclusion, Sarah felt a profound sense of transformation within herself. She had confronted her own shadows, acknowledged her mistakes, and sought forgiveness where it was needed. The mirror now reflected not only the complexities of her existence but also the potential for growth and renewal.

Elias placed a hand on her shoulder, his eyes filled with pride. "You have passed the trial, Sarah. You have shown the capacity for self-awareness, empathy, and growth. This experience will continue to shape your journey in the afterlife."

Sarah nodded, her heart filled with a sense of liberation and renewal. She understood that her journey was not just about self-discovery but also about the capacity for growth and transformation that resided within every soul.

And so, as she left the chamber of the Trial of Self-Reflection, Sarah carried with her a deeper understanding of herself and a renewed sense of purpose. The trial had tested her, challenged her, and ultimately allowed her to embrace the light and darkness within her own soul.

This extended Chapter 8 delves deeper into Sarah's challenging experience in the Trial of Self-Reflection within the afterlife. It highlights her introspection,

Chapter 9: The Realm of Transformation

As Sarah's journey through the afterlife continued, she found herself drawn to a realm unlike any she had encountered before—the Realm of Transformation. Guided by Elias, her trusted mentor, she entered a place of profound change and renewal, where the very essence of souls underwent a remarkable metamorphosis.

The realm was a surreal landscape, filled with vibrant colors and surreal landscapes that defied earthly description. It was as if the laws of physics and nature had been rewritten, allowing for endless possibilities of transformation. The air was charged with an electric energy that sent shivers of anticipation down Sarah's spine.

Elias spoke with a sense of reverence, "This is the Realm of Transformation, Sarah. Here, souls undergo a profound metamorphosis, shedding their old selves and emerging anew."

Sarah looked around, her eyes wide with wonder. "What kind of transformation takes place here?"

Elias gestured toward a shimmering pool of liquid light at the center of the realm. "Each soul's transformation is unique, reflecting their own desires, challenges, and aspirations. It is a process of shedding the layers of the past and embracing the potential for growth and renewal."

As Sarah approached the pool, she saw her reflection in the liquid light, but it was not her earthly self she saw—it was a vision of her highest potential, her truest essence. She saw herself as an artist, a healer, a friend, and a seeker of wisdom, all merged into one radiant being.

With a sense of determination, she stepped into the pool, feeling the liquid light envelop her. It was as if every cell in her body was being infused with a new energy, a sense of purpose and possibility. She felt herself shedding the weight of past regrets and limitations, and a profound sense of liberation washed over her.

As she emerged from the pool, she looked at herself with fresh eyes, feeling a deep sense of self-acceptance and love. She had undergone a transformation, not just in her appearance but in her essence. She had tapped into her highest potential, her true self.

Elias nodded with approval. "The Realm of Transformation allows you to connect with your true essence, to shed the limitations and fears that have held you back in life. It is a place of rebirth and renewal."

Over the following days, Sarah continued to explore the realm, witnessing the transformations of other souls. She saw a soul who had lived a life of fear and insecurity emerge as a being of courage and confidence. She saw a soul burdened by past traumas shed their pain and embrace a life of healing and compassion.

Each transformation was a testament to the resilience and potential of the soul, a reminder that growth and renewal were not just possible but inherent to the nature of existence.

One day, as she ventured deeper into the realm, she encountered a being of pure light—a soul who had undergone a transformation so profound that their radiance was blinding. Sarah could feel the energy and wisdom emanating from this being.

The radiant soul spoke with a voice that resonated with the harmony of the universe. "In the Realm of Transformation, we are given the gift of self-discovery and renewal. It is a place where the limitations of the past are shattered, and the infinite potential of the soul is revealed."

Sarah was humbled by the presence of this being, realizing

that her own transformation was just a glimpse of the boundless possibilities that lay before her. She felt a deep sense of gratitude for the opportunity to shed her old self and embrace her true essence.

As she continued to explore the realm, Sarah encountered a mirror, much like the one from the Trial of Self-Reflection, but with a profound difference. This mirror did not just reflect her current self but also showed glimpses of her potential future selves, each one representing a different path and destiny.

She saw herself as an artist, creating masterpieces that inspired and uplifted others. She saw herself as a healer, bringing comfort and healing to those in need. She saw herself as a mentor, guiding others on their journeys of self-discovery. And she saw herself as a seeker of wisdom, delving into the mysteries of existence.

Elias watched as Sarah contemplated the reflections in the mirror. "The Realm of Transformation offers you the opportunity to explore the infinite possibilities of your soul, Sarah. It is a reminder that your journey is not limited by the choices of the past but shaped by the choices of the present and the potential of the future."

Sarah nodded, feeling a sense of empowerment and purpose. She understood that her journey in the afterlife was not just about reflection and healing but also about embracing her true essence and potential. The Realm of Transformation had revealed the depths of her soul and the boundless horizons of her existence.

And so, as she left the realm behind, Sarah carried with her a renewed sense of purpose and a profound understanding of her own potential for growth and transformation. She knew that her journey was far from over, and that the afterlife held even greater revelations and challenges in store.

As Sarah left the Realm of Transformation behind, she felt a profound sense of renewal and purpose. The experiences she had encountered there had reshaped her understanding of her true self and her potential for growth. She knew that her journey in the afterlife was far from over, and that there were still mysteries and revelations to explore.

Guided by Elias, her trusted mentor, she embarked on a new path—one that would take her deeper into the heart of the afterlife and the essence of her own existence.

They walked through a landscape that seemed to shift and change with every step. Radiant colors danced in the air, and surreal vistas stretched out before them. It was a world of endless wonder and possibility, a place where the boundaries of reality and imagination blurred.

Elias spoke with a sense of anticipation, "We are now entering a realm known as the Heart of the Afterlife. It is a place where the very essence of existence is palpable, where the threads of consciousness intertwine."

Sarah looked around, her senses heightened by the energy of the realm. "What will we find here?"

Elias smiled, his eyes filled with a deep wisdom. "In the Heart of the Afterlife, you will find the answers to the most profound questions of existence. It is a place of revelation and awakening."

As they journeyed deeper into the realm, Sarah felt a

sensation of unity and interconnectedness that transcended anything she had ever experienced. She could sense the presence of other souls, not as separate entities, but as threads in the tapestry of consciousness.

She saw a soul who had once been a great philosopher, their thoughts and insights now part of the collective wisdom of the afterlife. She saw a soul who had once been a healer, their compassion and healing energy radiating throughout the realm. She saw souls who had lived lives of courage, creativity, and love, each contributing to the vibrant tapestry of existence.

Elias guided her to a shimmering pool of light at the center of the realm. It seemed to pulse with a rhythmic energy, like the heartbeat of the afterlife itself. Sarah gazed into the pool, feeling a sense of connection to the very essence of existence.

"The Heart of the Afterlife is a place of profound insight and revelation," Elias explained. "It is here that you can gain a deeper understanding of the nature of consciousness, the interconnectedness of all souls, and the purpose of existence."

Sarah watched as images and symbols began to form in the pool, each one representing a facet of the mysteries of existence. She saw the image of a tree with roots that extended deep into the earth, symbolizing the connection between the physical and spiritual realms. She saw a spiral, representing the eternal cycle of growth and renewal. And she saw a radiant sun, signifying the source of all consciousness and light.

As she gazed into the pool, Sarah felt a profound sense of clarity and understanding wash over her. She realized that the afterlife was not just a destination but a journey of the soul, a continuous exploration of consciousness and evolution.

Elias placed a hand on her shoulder, his presence a source of strength and guidance. "In the Heart of the Afterlife, you can gain insights into your own purpose and the role you play in the grand tapestry of existence. It is a place of awakening, where the deepest truths of the soul are revealed."

Sarah nodded, her heart filled with a sense of purpose and wonder. She understood that her journey in the afterlife was a quest for knowledge, a search for meaning, and a commitment to growth and transformation.

As they continued to explore the Heart of the Afterlife, Sarah encountered other souls who were also seeking answers and revelations. They shared stories of their own journeys, their insights, and the profound moments of awakening they had experienced.

One soul, a poet who had once written words of beauty and inspiration, spoke of the power of creativity and expression in the afterlife. They explained how the act of creation was a reflection of the soul's desire to explore and communicate its deepest truths.

Another soul, a philosopher who had pondered the mysteries of existence in life, engaged Sarah in a deep conversation about the nature of consciousness and the interconnectedness of all souls. They discussed the idea that every soul's journey contributed to the collective evolution of consciousness.

As the hours passed, Sarah felt a sense of unity and purpose that transcended her earthly understanding. She realized that her journey was not just about self-discovery but also about contributing to the greater tapestry of existence. Every insight, every revelation, added to the collective wisdom of the afterlife.

And so, as she left the Heart of the Afterlife behind, Sarah carried with her a renewed sense of purpose and a profound understanding of the interconnectedness of all souls. She knew that her journey was far from over, and that the mysteries of existence continued to beckon.

Chapter 10 The Tapestry of Souls

As Sarah's journey through the afterlife continued, she and Elias ventured into a realm known as the Tapestry of Souls. It was a place where the stories and experiences of all souls were interwoven into a magnificent and ever-changing fabric of existence.

The landscape of the Tapestry of Souls was a breathtaking display of color and light. Vast threads of energy stretched out before them, each one representing the unique journey of a soul. The threads wove together in intricate patterns, creating a living tapestry that pulsed with the energy of countless lives.

Elias spoke with reverence, "This is the Tapestry of Souls, Sarah. It is a reflection of the interconnectedness of all existence. Here, you can witness the stories and experiences of every soul who has ever lived."

Sarah gazed in awe at the swirling threads of energy. It was as if she could see the entire history of humanity and beyond, from the earliest moments of consciousness to the present and beyond. She saw moments of joy and moments of sorrow, moments of love and moments of conflict, all woven into the fabric of existence.

Elias gestured to a particular thread, one that seemed to shimmer with a radiant intensity. "Let us follow this thread, Sarah. It represents the journey of a soul who has had a profound impact on the world."

As they followed the thread, Sarah felt herself drawn into the life and experiences of the soul it represented. She saw a woman who had dedicated her life to social justice and equality, a soul who had fought tirelessly for the rights of the marginalized and oppressed.

She witnessed moments of courage as the soul stood up to injustice, moments of compassion as she reached out to those in need, and moments of determination as she never wavered in her commitment to create a more just and equitable world.

Sarah felt a deep sense of connection to the soul's journey, as if she could feel the emotions and experiences as if they were her own. She understood that the Tapestry of Souls was not just a reflection of individual stories but also a reminder of the collective journey of humanity.

Elias spoke softly, "In the Tapestry of Souls, you can gain insights into the interconnectedness of all existence. Every action, every choice, has a ripple effect that extends far beyond the individual soul. It is a reminder of the profound impact each soul can have on the world."

As they continued to follow the threads of the tapestry, Sarah saw a thread that seemed to shimmer with a golden light. It represented the journey of a soul who had devoted their life to the pursuit of knowledge and wisdom. She watched as the soul delved into the mysteries of the universe, seeking to unlock the secrets of existence.

The soul's journey took them to ancient libraries of wisdom, to conversations with sages and scholars, and to moments of profound insight and revelation. Sarah felt a sense of kinship with the soul's quest for knowledge, a reminder of her own thirst for understanding.

Elias nodded, his eyes filled with understanding. "The Tapestry of Souls is a place of reflection and illumination, Sarah. It allows you to witness the diverse paths and experiences of all souls, and to gain insights into the collective wisdom of existence."

As they explored further, Sarah saw a thread that seemed to vibrate with a powerful energy. It represented the journey of a soul who had dedicated their life to the exploration of creativity and artistry. She watched as the soul expressed their innermost thoughts and emotions through music, painting, and dance.

The soul's creations touched the hearts of those who encountered them, inspiring joy, awe, and a sense of connection. Sarah felt a deep resonance with the soul's expression of creativity, a reminder of her own love for art and self-expression.

Elias spoke with a smile, "In the Tapestry of Souls, you can witness the beauty and diversity of human creativity. It is a celebration of the unique gifts and talents that each soul possesses."

As they continued to explore the tapestry, Sarah felt a sense of wonder and gratitude for the opportunity to witness the stories and experiences of all souls. She realized that the afterlife was not just a place of reflection and self-discovery but also a place of connection and unity.

One day, as they followed a particularly intricate thread, Sarah noticed something remarkable. The threads of the tapestry were not static but were constantly shifting and changing, creating new patterns and connections. It was as if the tapestry itself was a living, breathing entity, evolving and adapting with the collective consciousness of all souls.

Elias nodded in acknowledgment. "The Tapestry of Souls is not a static representation but a reflection of the ongoing evolution of consciousness. It reminds us that existence is a dynamic and ever-changing journey."

As Sarah stood before the mesmerizing tapestry, she felt a sense of peace and purpose wash over her. She understood that her own journey was just one thread in the vast tapestry of existence, a part of the greater whole. She realized that every choice, every action, had the potential to create ripples of change that extended far beyond her own life.

Elias placed a hand on her shoulder, his presence a source of comfort and guidance. "The Tapestry of Souls is a reminder that every soul is interconnected, that the choices and experiences of one soul can impact the collective consciousness of all existence. It is a celebration of the unity and diversity of the human experience."

Sarah nodded, her heart filled with a profound sense of gratitude and understanding. She knew that her journey in the afterlife was not just a personal quest for self-discovery but also a contribution to the greater tapestry of existence. She felt a deep sense of purpose and unity with all souls who had ever lived.

And so, as she and Elias continued to explore the Tapestry

of Souls, Sarah carried with her a renewed sense of connection and purpose. She knew that her journey was far from over, and that the mysteries of existence continued to unfold before her.:

Chapter 11: The Garden of Reflection

As Sarah's journey through the afterlife unfolded, she and Elias ventured into a realm known as the Garden of Reflection. It was a place of serene beauty and contemplation, where souls could find solace, healing, and profound insights into their life's journey.

The Garden of Reflection was a lush oasis of vibrant flora, each plant radiating a gentle, soothing light. The air was filled with a sweet, fragrant scent, and the atmosphere resonated with a sense of tranquility. It was a sanctuary for souls seeking moments of introspection and understanding.

Elias spoke with a soft voice, "This is the Garden of Reflection, Sarah. It is a place where souls can find clarity, heal old wounds, and gain deeper insights into their earthly experiences."

Sarah looked around, her eyes taking in the beauty of the garden. She noticed that each plant seemed to have a unique energy, as if it held the wisdom and experiences of a soul. It was a living garden of stories and memories waiting to be explored.

"What will we find here?" Sarah asked, her curiosity piqued.

Elias smiled, his presence a source of comfort. "In the Garden of Reflection, you can explore the memories and emotions that have shaped your journey. It is a place of healing and self-discovery."

As they strolled along a winding path, they approached a tree with leaves that shimmered like emerald jewels. The tree seemed to beckon Sarah, and as she reached out to touch its leaves, she felt a rush of emotions and memories flood her senses.

She saw moments from her childhood, moments of laughter and play, moments of innocence and wonder. She saw the loving embrace of her parents, the wisdom of her grandparents, and the friendships that had sustained her through the years. The tree whispered to her the importance of cherishing the beauty and simplicity of life.

Tears welled up in Sarah's eyes as she relived these cherished memories. It was as if the tree had unlocked a hidden chamber of her heart, allowing her to reconnect with the pure and joyful moments of her past.

Elias nodded in understanding. "The Garden of Reflection allows you to revisit the memories that have shaped your journey. It is a reminder of the beauty and significance of the experiences that have molded you."

As they continued their journey through the garden, Sarah encountered a pond with crystal-clear waters. As she gazed into the pond, she saw reflections of moments of challenge and adversity from her life. She saw the times when she had faced uncertainty, doubt, and fear.

The reflections in the pond showed her the strength and resilience she had demonstrated in those moments. She realized that even in the face of difficulties, she had found the courage to keep moving forward, to learn and grow from her experiences.

Elias spoke with pride, "The Garden of Reflection also allows you to confront the challenges and trials of your journey. It is a place of healing and transformation, where you can gain insights into your own strength and resilience."

As they ventured deeper into the garden, Sarah came across a meadow filled with a multitude of flowers, each one representing a different emotion and experience from her life. There were flowers of joy, sorrow, love, and forgiveness, each one radiating its unique energy.

Sarah reached out to touch one of the flowers, and she felt an overwhelming surge of emotion. It was a flower of gratitude, a reminder of the countless blessings and moments of grace that had graced her life. She realized that even in the midst of challenges, there had always been reasons to be thankful.

Elias spoke softly, "In the Garden of Reflection, you can explore the full spectrum of emotions that have enriched your journey. It is a place of healing and acceptance, where you can embrace the complexity of your own experiences."

As they wandered further, they arrived at a grove of ancient trees, their gnarled roots reaching deep into the earth. The trees seemed to exude a sense of wisdom and resilience, as if they had witnessed the passage of countless ages.

Sarah touched one of the trees, and suddenly, she felt a connection to the collective wisdom of all souls. She saw the interconnectedness of her own journey with the journeys of others, a reminder that she was never alone in her experiences.

Elias nodded in affirmation. "The Garden of Reflection is a place of unity and connection, Sarah. It allows you to explore the interconnectedness of all existence and gain insights from the collective wisdom of souls."

As they continued to explore the garden, Sarah realized that it was not just a place of reflection but also a place of healing and renewal. Each element of the garden—the tree, the pond, the meadow, and the grove of ancient trees—offered a unique opportunity for self-discovery and growth.

One day, as they sat beneath the shade of a majestic tree, Sarah closed her eyes and allowed herself to be enveloped by the tranquility of the garden. She felt a deep sense of peace and acceptance wash over her, as if the garden itself was whispering words of comfort and reassurance.

Elias spoke softly, "The Garden of Reflection is a place where you can find solace and healing, Sarah. It is here that you can come to terms with the complexities of your earthly journey and find inner peace."

Sarah nodded in gratitude, her heart filled with a sense of serenity she had never known before. She understood that the garden was a sanctuary for the soul, a place where she could release the burdens of the past and embrace the beauty of the present.

As the days passed in the Garden of Reflection, Sarah began to notice subtle changes within herself. She felt a deep sense of inner healing, as if old wounds were being gently tended to and transformed into sources of strength. She realized that the garden was not just a place of introspection but also a place of profound healing and renewal.

One evening, as they sat by a tranquil pond, Elias spoke about the power of forgiveness. "Forgiveness is a key that can unlock the doors to healing, Sarah. It is a gift you can give to others and to yourself. Is there someone you need to forgive?"

Sarah closed her eyes and thought about her earthly life. She recalled moments of hurt and betrayal, moments when she had felt wronged by others. And she realized that holding onto these grievances had only weighed her down.

With a deep breath, she whispered, "I forgive. I release these grievances and choose to let go of the pain they have caused."

As she uttered these words, she felt a profound sense of release and lightness. It was as if a heavy burden had been lifted from her heart, allowing her to breathe freely and deeply.

Elias smiled, his eyes filled with warmth. "Forgiveness is a powerful act of self-liberation, Sarah. It allows you to free yourself from the chains of resentment and anger, and to embrace the peace and healing that forgiveness brings."

With each passing day in the Garden of Reflection, Sarah gained deeper insights into her own journey and the importance of self-compassion. She realized that her earthly life had been a tapestry of experiences, each one contributing to her growth and evolution as a soul.

One morning, as she sat amidst the flowers in the meadow, she felt a sense of gratitude welling up within her. She thought about the people who had touched her life, the moments of joy and love, and the opportunities for growth that had come her way.

With tears of gratitude in her eyes, she whispered, "Thank you for the gift of life. Thank you for the lessons and the love."

The flowers seemed to respond, their petals glowing with

a radiant light. It was as if the garden itself was echoing her sentiments, reminding her of the beauty and significance of her earthly journey.

Elias nodded in affirmation. "Gratitude is a powerful force for transformation, Sarah. It allows you to recognize the blessings in your life and to open your heart to even greater abundance."

As her time in the Garden of Reflection continued, Sarah began to sense a deep connection with all souls who had journeyed through the afterlife. She realized that they were all on a shared quest for understanding, healing, and growth. It was a journey of unity and interconnectedness.

One evening, as they watched the sun set over the garden, Elias spoke about the interconnectedness of all existence. "In the grand tapestry of existence, every soul plays a unique role, and every experience contributes to the collective evolution of consciousness."

Sarah gazed at the setting sun, its golden light casting a warm glow over the garden. She felt a profound sense of unity with all souls who had ever lived, a sense of shared purpose and journey.

She whispered, "We are all connected, aren't we? Our journeys are intertwined, and our experiences shape the tapestry of existence."

Elias smiled, his presence a source of wisdom and guidance. "Yes, Sarah. In the Garden of Reflection, you can gain insights into the interconnectedness of all souls and the beauty of the collective journey."

As the days turned into weeks in the Garden of Reflection,

Sarah knew that her time there was coming to an end. She had gained profound insights into her own journey and the interconnectedness of all existence. She had healed old wounds, embraced forgiveness, and found inner peace.

One morning, as she stood beneath the shade of a tree, Elias spoke with a sense of gentle encouragement. "It is time to continue your journey, Sarah. The afterlife has much more to offer, and your path leads to new horizons of discovery and growth."

Sarah nodded, her heart filled with gratitude for the healing and insights she had gained in the garden. She knew that her journey was far from over, and that the mysteries of existence continued to beckon.

And so, as she left the Garden of Reflection behind, Sarah carried with her a renewed sense of inner peace and a profound understanding of the power of healing, forgiveness, and gratitude. She knew that her journey in the afterlife was a quest for self-discovery and unity with all souls who had ever lived.

Chapter 12: The River of Wisdom

After leaving the Garden of Reflection, Sarah and Elias embarked on a new phase of their journey through the afterlife. They found themselves standing at the edge of a vast and serene river known as the River of Wisdom.

The river's waters shimmered with a soft, iridescent glow, and a gentle breeze rustled the leaves of the surrounding trees. It was a place of serenity and contemplation, where souls could come to gain deeper insights into the mysteries of existence.

Elias spoke with a sense of reverence, "This is the River of Wisdom, Sarah. It is a place where the waters of knowledge flow, carrying with them the collective wisdom of all souls who have ever lived."

Sarah looked out at the tranquil river, her eyes drawn to the gentle ripples on its surface. She felt a deep sense of anticipation, a knowing that this river held profound insights waiting to be discovered.

"What will we find here?" she asked, her voice filled with curiosity.

Elias smiled, his presence a source of comfort. "In the River of Wisdom, you can immerse yourself in the collective knowledge of all existence. It is a place of reflection and enlightenment."

As they approached the river, Sarah noticed that it was not just water but a living flow of energy. She extended her hand to touch the waters, and as her fingertips made contact, she felt a surge of awareness rush through her.

Images and symbols began to form in her mind, each one representing a facet of the river's wisdom. She saw the image of an ancient book, its pages filled with the stories and insights of countless souls. She saw a tree of knowledge, its roots reaching deep into the earth and its branches stretching toward the heavens. And she saw a radiant sun, symbolizing the source of all wisdom and light.

Elias watched as Sarah absorbed the river's energy. "The River of Wisdom is a place of revelation and enlightenment, Sarah. It allows you to gain deeper insights into the nature of existence and the mysteries of consciousness."

As they stepped into the river, Sarah felt a profound sense of connection to the collective wisdom of all souls. It was as if she could hear the whispers of countless voices, each one offering a piece of the puzzle that made up the grand tapestry of existence.

She closed her eyes and allowed herself to be carried by the gentle current of the river. As she surrendered to the flow, she began to experience moments of clarity and understanding that transcended her earthly knowledge.

She saw visions of ancient civilizations, their wisdom and knowledge passed down through the ages. She witnessed the discoveries of scientists and philosophers, their quest for understanding shaping the course of human history. She felt the insights of poets and artists, their creations inspired by the depths of the human soul.

Elias spoke softly, "In the River of Wisdom, you can explore the collective knowledge of humanity and gain insights into the eternal truths that have guided souls throughout time."

As they continued to float along the river, Sarah encountered a particularly vibrant section where the waters seemed to dance with a playful energy. She watched as the river transformed into a kaleidoscope of colors, each hue representing a different branch of knowledge and wisdom.

She saw the color blue, symbolizing the wisdom of the oceans and the mysteries of the deep. She saw the color green, representing the knowledge of the natural world and the interconnectedness of all life. She saw the color gold, signifying the wisdom of the ages and the quest for spiritual enlightenment.

Sarah reached out to touch the colorful waters, and as her fingers made contact, she felt a surge of insight and inspiration. It was as if the river itself was offering her gifts of knowledge and understanding.

Elias nodded in acknowledgment. "The River of Wisdom is a place of inspiration and creativity, Sarah. It allows you to tap into the boundless wellspring of knowledge and insight that exists within the collective consciousness of all souls."

As they journeyed further along the river, Sarah encountered a section where the waters seemed to flow through a dense forest of ancient trees. Each tree bore markings and symbols that represented different cultures and traditions from throughout history.

She saw the symbols of ancient civilizations, their languages and art forms preserved in the annals of time. She saw the symbols of indigenous cultures, their deep connection to the earth and the cycles of nature. She saw the symbols of spiritual traditions, their teachings and practices guiding souls toward enlightenment.

Sarah reached out to trace the symbols on the trees, and as her fingers moved over the rough bark, she felt a profound sense of reverence and understanding. It was as if the wisdom of these ancient cultures was being imparted to her, offering insights into the richness of human history and spirituality.

Elias spoke with a sense of awe, "The River of Wisdom allows you to explore the cultural and spiritual diversity of humanity, Sarah. It is a reminder that the quest for knowledge and enlightenment is a universal and timeless journey."

As they continued to float along the river, Sarah noticed

that the waters began to take on a different quality. They became more transparent, as if she could see through the surface into the depths below.

She gazed down and saw glimpses of the past and future intertwined, moments of history and moments yet to come. It was as if time itself was a river, with its currents flowing in both directions.

Elias explained, "In this part of the River of Wisdom, you can gain insights into the nature of time and the interconnectedness of past, present, and future. It is a place of profound understanding and awareness."

Sarah watched as the images of the past and future continued to unfold before her. She saw moments of great change and transformation, moments of challenge and triumph. She realized that time was not a linear progression but a tapestry of experiences, each one shaping the next.

Elias placed a hand on her shoulder, his presence a source of guidance and support. "The River of Wisdom offers you a glimpse into the eternal nature of existence, Sarah. It is a reminder that the journey of the soul transcends the limitations of time and space."

As they approached the end of their journey along the river, Sarah felt a sense of profound gratitude for the insights and wisdom she had gained. She knew that her journey in the afterlife was a quest for understanding and self-discovery, a journey that continued to unfold before her.

Elias spoke with a smile, "The River of Wisdom has offered you a glimpse into the boundless wellspring of knowledge and insight that exists within the collective consciousness of all souls. It is a reminder that the quest for wisdom and understanding is a never-ending journey."

Sarah nodded in agreement, her heart filled with a sense of wonder and reverence for the river's wisdom. She understood that her journey in the afterlife was far from over, and that the mysteries of existence continued to beckon.

And so, as she and Elias left the River of Wisdom behind, Sarah carried with her a renewed sense of understanding and insight. She knew that her journey was a quest for knowledge and enlightenment, a journey that would lead her to even greater revelations and challenges in the afterlife.

Chapter 13: The Library of Eternity

As Sarah and Elias continued their journey through the afterlife, they found themselves standing before a magnificent structure that stretched toward the heavens—an awe-inspiring library known as the Library of Eternity.

The library's towering spires seemed to touch the very sky, and its grand doors stood wide open, inviting souls to enter. The air around it was charged with an energy that hinted at the vast knowledge and wisdom contained within its walls.

Elias spoke with a sense of reverence, "This is the Library of Eternity, Sarah. It is a place where the accumulated knowledge and wisdom of all souls are preserved. Here, you can explore the boundless depths of understanding."

Sarah looked up at the towering library in awe, her heart filled with anticipation. She had always been a lover of books and knowledge, and the prospect of delving into the collective wisdom of all existence filled her with excitement.

"What will we find here?" she asked, her voice trembling with eagerness.

Elias smiled, his presence a source of reassurance. "In the Library of Eternity, you can embark on a journey through the written and unwritten knowledge of all souls. It is a place of discovery and enlightenment."

As they entered the library, Sarah was greeted by the sight of endless shelves, each one filled with books, scrolls, and manuscripts of all shapes and sizes. The shelves stretched out in every direction, disappearing into the horizon.

Sarah's eyes sparkled with wonder as she reached out to touch one of the books. As her fingers brushed the ancient pages, she felt a rush of energy and insight. It was as if the knowledge contained within the book was being absorbed into her very being.

Elias gestured toward the vast expanse of the library. "The Library of Eternity holds the writings and thoughts of all souls who have ever lived. Here, you can explore the diverse perspectives, ideas, and wisdom that have shaped human and spiritual understanding."

Sarah began her exploration by selecting a book from one of the shelves. It was a volume filled with the writings of a philosopher from a distant age, a soul who had pondered the nature of reality and existence.

As she read the philosopher's words, she felt a profound resonance with their thoughts. It was as if the philosopher's insights were speaking directly to her soul, illuminating the mysteries of the universe in ways she had never imagined.

Elias watched as Sarah delved deeper into the philosopher's

writings. "The Library of Eternity allows you to gain insights from the minds and hearts of all souls, Sarah. It is a place where you can expand your understanding of the cosmos and the nature of consciousness."

As she continued to explore, Sarah encountered books on a wide range of topics. She read about the mysteries of the cosmos, the intricacies of quantum physics, and the nature of time and space. She delved into the writings of poets and artists, whose words and creations touched the depths of the human soul.

She immersed herself in the wisdom of ancient sages and modern thinkers, each one offering a unique perspective on the human experience and the quest for spiritual enlightenment. It was a journey through the rich tapestry of human knowledge and understanding.

One day, as she sat amidst a sea of books, Sarah came across a volume that seemed to glow with a radiant light. It was a book of ancient prophecies and visions, written by a soul who had glimpsed the future of humanity.

As she read the prophecies, Sarah felt a sense of awe and wonder. The visions spoke of a time of awakening and transformation, a time when humanity would come to realize its interconnectedness and its potential for greatness.

Elias nodded in acknowledgment. "The Library of Eternity holds not only the knowledge of the past but also glimpses of the future, Sarah. It is a reminder that the journey of the soul extends beyond the boundaries of time and space."

As Sarah continued to explore the library, she began to notice that the books and scrolls seemed to respond to her thoughts and questions. When she wondered about the nature of consciousness, a book on neuroscience and spirituality appeared before her. When she pondered the mysteries of the afterlife, a scroll containing the writings of souls who had journeyed beyond life and death materialized in her hands.

Elias explained, "The Library of Eternity is a place of interactive learning, Sarah. It responds to the inquiries and curiosities of the soul, offering insights and knowledge tailored to your quest for understanding."

Sarah marveled at the library's ability to provide answers to her deepest questions and to guide her on her journey of self-discovery. She realized that the library was not just a repository of knowledge but a living source of wisdom and enlightenment.

One evening, as she sat in a quiet corner of the library, she began to reflect on her own journey through the afterlife. She thought about the insights and experiences she had gained, the moments of healing and transformation, and the profound sense of unity she had discovered.

With a sense of gratitude in her heart, she whispered a silent prayer of thanks to the universe and all the souls who had guided her on her path.

Elias, who had been silently observing, spoke with a smile, "Your journey in the afterlife is a testament to the power of self-discovery and the quest for wisdom, Sarah. It is a reminder that the soul's journey is a continuous exploration of consciousness and growth."

Sarah nodded in agreement, her heart filled with a deep sense of purpose and wonder. She understood that her journey in the afterlife was not just about gaining knowledge but also about contributing to the collective wisdom of all souls who had ever lived.

As she continued to explore the library, she encountered a section that held books and scrolls filled with stories and experiences from the lives of souls who had journeyed through the afterlife. She read about the challenges they had faced, the insights they had gained, and the moments of profound transformation they had experienced.

Elias explained, "The Library of Eternity also contains the stories and experiences of all souls who have explored the afterlife, Sarah. It is a place where you can connect with the journeys and insights of your fellow travelers."

Sarah felt a sense of kinship with the souls whose stories she encountered. She realized that their experiences mirrored her own journey of self-discovery and growth. It was a reminder that the afterlife was a shared realm, where souls supported and learned from each other.

As the days turned into weeks in the Library of Eternity, Sarah knew that her time there was coming to an end. She had gained profound insights into the nature of existence, the mysteries of consciousness, and the interconnectedness of all souls.

Elias spoke with a sense of gentle encouragement, "It is time to continue your journey, Sarah. The afterlife has more to offer, and your path leads to new horizons of discovery and growth."

Sarah nodded in acknowledgment, her heart filled with gratitude for the knowledge and wisdom she had gained in the library. She knew that her journey was far from over, and that the mysteries of existence continued to beckon.

And so, as she left the Library of Eternity behind, Sarah carried with her a renewed sense of understanding and enlightenment. She knew that her journey in the afterlife was a quest for self-discovery and the continuous exploration of consciousness and knowledge

Chapter 14: The Temple of Reflection

After leaving the Library of Eternity, Sarah and Elias continued their journey through the afterlife, guided by an unending sense of wonder and curiosity. Their path led them to a place of profound significance—the Temple of Reflection.

The Temple stood atop a hill, bathed in a soft, ethereal light that seemed to radiate from within. Its architecture was a testament to the grandeur of the afterlife, with intricate carvings and ornate columns that reached toward the heavens.

Elias spoke with a hushed reverence, "This is the Temple of Reflection, Sarah. It is a place of deep introspection and self-discovery. Here, souls come to confront their innermost truths and gain insights into the essence of their being."

Sarah looked up at the majestic temple, her heart filled with anticipation. She had journeyed through realms of knowledge and wisdom, and now, the prospect of exploring the depths of her own soul was both thrilling and humbling.

"What will we find here?" she asked, her voice filled with a mixture of excitement and trepidation.

Elias smiled, his presence a source of unwavering support. "In the Temple of Reflection, you can delve into the essence of your own soul, confront your deepest fears and desires, and gain a profound understanding of your unique journey."

As they entered the temple, Sarah was greeted by a sense of tranquility that seemed to envelop her like a warm embrace. The interior of the temple was adorned with soft candlelight and intricate mosaics that depicted the phases of the moon, symbolizing the cycles of reflection and transformation.

In the center of the temple stood a luminous pool of water, its surface as still as a mirror. It seemed to beckon Sarah, inviting her to gaze into its depths and explore the mysteries within.

Elias led her to the edge of the pool, his voice a soothing presence. "The pool of reflection is a portal to the innermost chambers of your soul, Sarah. It is a place where you can confront your past, embrace your present, and envision your future."

Sarah peered into the pool and watched as images and memories from her earthly life began to surface. She saw moments of joy and moments of sorrow, moments of love and moments of loss. Each image seemed to dance upon the water's surface, telling the story of her life.

As she continued to gaze into the pool, she saw moments of choice and moments of consequence. She witnessed the impact of her actions on others and the ripple effect of her decisions. It was a journey through the tapestry of her own existence.

Elias spoke softly, "The pool of reflection allows you to revisit the moments and choices that have shaped your journey, Sarah. It is a place of healing and understanding."

With a sense of courage, Sarah began to explore the images and memories that emerged from the pool. She saw moments of growth and moments of challenge, moments of self-discovery and moments of doubt.

She saw the times when she had faced her fears and emerged stronger, and she saw the times when she had faltered and learned valuable lessons. It was a journey through the depths of her own soul, a journey toward self-acceptance and understanding.

Elias watched as Sarah confronted her own truths with courage and grace. "The Temple of Reflection is a place of profound self-discovery, Sarah. It allows you to embrace the complexity of your own experiences and find healing and acceptance."

As Sarah continued to explore the pool of reflection, she noticed that the water's surface began to shift and change, revealing visions of her present and future. She saw glimpses of the afterlife and the limitless possibilities it held.

She saw herself connecting with other souls, sharing wisdom and insights, and contributing to the collective con-sciousness of all existence. She realized that her journey in the afterlife was not just a personal quest for self-discovery but also a contribution to the greater tapestry of existence.

Elias spoke with a sense of affirmation, "The Temple of Reflection allows you to envision your future and embrace the infinite potential of your soul, Sarah. It is a place of inspiration and transformation."

With newfound clarity and purpose, Sarah felt a deep sense of gratitude for the opportunity to explore the depths of her own soul. She knew that her journey was far from over, and that the mysteries of existence continued to unfold before her.

One day, as she sat in quiet contemplation within the temple, she felt a presence beside her—a presence that emanated a profound sense of love and guidance. She turned to see a luminous figure, radiant with light and grace.

The figure spoke with a voice that resonated with wisdom and compassion. "I am a guardian of the Temple of Reflection, Sarah. I am here to assist you on your journey of self-discovery and transformation."

Sarah felt a deep sense of trust and connection with the guardian. She realized that this encounter was not a mere coincidence but a profound moment of guidance and support.

With a sense of humility, she asked, "What wisdom do you have to share with me?"

The guardian smiled, their presence filling the temple with a gentle radiance. "In the depths of your soul, Sarah, you hold the key to your own transformation. Embrace your past with gratitude, your present with awareness, and your future with boundless potential."

As Sarah absorbed the guardian's words, she felt a profound sense of empowerment and clarity. She understood that her journey in the afterlife was a journey toward self-acceptance, growth, and the realization of her true potential.

Elias nodded in affirmation, his presence a source of encouragement. "The Temple of Reflection is a place of empowerment, Sarah. It allows you to confront your own truths and envision the path of your soul's evolution."

With a renewed sense of purpose, Sarah continued her exploration of the Temple of Reflection. She found herself drawn to a series of ornate doors that seemed to radiate a sense of mystery and promise. As she approached them, she realized that each door led to a chamber of the temple, each one representing a different aspect of her soul's journey.

The first door she entered led to a chamber filled with mirrors of various shapes and sizes. Each mirror reflected a different aspect of herself—the joyful, the wounded, the courageous, the curious. Sarah gazed into each mirror, seeing the facets of her own soul with compassion and acceptance. She realized that self-love and self-acceptance were key to her inner transformation.

The second door opened into a chamber adorned with paintings and murals that depicted pivotal moments from her earthly life. She saw moments of challenge and moments of triumph, moments of connection and moments of solitude. It was a visual narrative of her journey, and as she studied each painting, she gained a deeper understanding of the lessons and blessings of her life.

The third door led to a chamber filled with the soothing sound of flowing water. In the center of the chamber was a tranquil pool, much like the one at the entrance of the temple. But this pool was special—it held reflections of her dreams and aspirations. Sarah gazed into the pool, seeing images of her future self, of the person she aspired to become. It was a reminder that her journey was a continuous evolution toward her highest potential.

The fourth door revealed a chamber illuminated by a soft,

radiant light. In the center of the room was a luminous crystal that seemed to pulse with energy. Sarah approached the crystal and placed her hand upon it. She felt a surge of insight and intuition flow through her. It was a chamber of intuition and inner guidance, a reminder that her inner wisdom was a powerful compass on her journey.

Elias watched as Sarah explored the chambers of the temple with a sense of curiosity and self-discovery. "The Temple of Reflection allows you to explore the multi-dimensional aspects of your own soul, Sarah. It is a place where you can integrate your past, embrace your present, and envision your future."

As Sarah continued her journey through the temple, she encountered a series of passages and corridors that seemed to lead deeper into the heart of her own consciousness. Each passage held its own challenges and revelations, testing her resolve and pushing her to confront her own truths.

In one passage, she faced a shadowy figure that seemed to embody her deepest fears and insecurities. The figure taunted her with doubts and uncertainties, but Sarah, fortified by her journey of self-reflection, found the inner strength to confront and dispel these shadows.

In another passage, she encountered a series of mirrors that reflected her own judgments and self-criticism. She realized that these judgments were barriers to her own growth and self-acceptance. With courage and self-compassion, she shattered the mirrors, liberating herself from self-imposed limitations.

In yet another passage, she found herself in a chamber

filled with the sound of her own inner voice—the voice that had guided her through moments of doubt and confusion, the voice of intuition and wisdom. She listened to her inner guidance, trusting that it would lead her toward her highest potential.

Elias spoke with pride, "The Temple of Reflection challenges you to confront your own limitations and fears, Sarah. It is a place of empowerment and transformation, where you can emerge stronger and more self-aware."

As Sarah emerged from the deepest chambers of the temple, she felt a profound sense of transformation and renewal. She had confronted her own truths, embraced her past with gratitude, and envisioned her future with boundless potential. She understood that her journey in the afterlife was a continuous evolution of consciousness and self-discovery.

One evening, as she sat in quiet contemplation within the temple, she felt a presence beside her—a presence that emanated a profound sense of peace and fulfillment. It was the guardian of the temple, their luminous form radiating a sense of completeness.

The guardian spoke with a voice that resonated with wisdom and love. "You have journeyed deep within the chambers of your own soul, Sarah. You have confronted your own truths and embraced your own potential. It is time to carry this wisdom and transformation forward on your journey."

Sarah nodded in gratitude, her heart filled with a deep sense of fulfillment. She knew that her journey in the afterlife was a testament to the power of self-discovery and the continuous exploration of consciousness.

With a sense of purpose and self-acceptance, she left the Temple of Reflection behind, carrying with her a renewed understanding of her own soul and the infinite possibilities that lay before her.

And so, as Sarah and Elias continued their journey through the afterlife, they knew that the mysteries of existence continued to beckon. The temple had been a place of profound self-discovery and transformation, a reminder that the soul's journey was a continuous exploration of consciousness and growth.

Chapter 15: The Realm of Dreams

After leaving the Temple of Reflection, Sarah and Elias embarked on a new phase of their journey through the afterlife. Their path led them to a realm of enchantment and mystery—the Realm of Dreams.

This realm seemed to stretch endlessly in all directions, with ethereal landscapes that shifted and transformed like the contents of a dream. Colors swirled and blended in mesmerizing patterns, and the air was filled with a gentle, melodic hum that seemed to resonate with the very essence of existence.

Elias spoke with a sense of wonder, "Welcome to the Realm of Dreams, Sarah. This is a place where the boundaries of reality and imagination are blurred, where the dreams of souls take shape and come to life."

Sarah looked around in awe, her senses overwhelmed by the beauty and fluidity of this realm. She had entered a world where dreams and imagination held sway, and the possibilities seemed limitless.

"What will we find here?" she asked, her voice filled with curiosity.

Elias smiled, his presence a source of guidance and reassurance. "In the Realm of Dreams, you can explore the dreams and aspirations of all souls, gain insights into the power of creativity and imagination, and experience the boundless potential of consciousness."

As they ventured deeper into the realm, Sarah realized that the landscapes and scenery were shaped by the thoughts and desires of the souls who passed through. She watched as trees sprouted from the ground, their leaves forming intricate patterns of color. She saw rivers that flowed with liquid light, and mountains that shimmered like precious gems.

Elias explained, "In the Realm of Dreams, the very fabric of reality is shaped by the collective dreams and intentions of all souls. It is a reminder of the creative power that resides within each soul."

Sarah marveled at the idea that the landscape around her was a reflection of the dreams and intentions of all souls who had ever lived. It was a testament to the interconnectedness of all existence, where individual dreams merged into a tapestry of collective creation.

As they continued to explore, Sarah noticed that the realm was filled with beings of light and energy, each one embodying a different dream or aspiration. She saw beings of joy and laughter, beings of healing and compassion, and beings of inspiration and innovation.

She approached one of these beings, a radiant figure whose

presence exuded a sense of serenity and contentment. "What is your dream?" she asked.

The being smiled, its energy dancing with light. "My dream is to bring peace and harmony to all souls, to help them find the serenity within their own hearts."

Sarah felt a sense of resonance with the being's dream. She realized that the realm was not just a place of dreams but also a place of connection, where souls could share their dreams and aspirations, and find support and inspiration from one another.

Elias nodded in affirmation, "In the Realm of Dreams, you can connect with the dreams and intentions of all souls, Sarah. It is a place of unity and shared vision."

As they journeyed further into the realm, Sarah began to notice that she could shape the environment with her own thoughts and intentions. She experimented with her creative power, and to her amazement, she saw flowers bloom at her command, and stars form constellations in the sky.

Elias encouraged her exploration, "The Realm of Dreams is a place where your own creative potential is magnified, Sarah. It is a reminder that the power of imagination and intention can shape your reality."

With newfound understanding, Sarah realized that she could use her creative abilities to not only shape the landscape but also to explore her own dreams and aspirations. She closed her eyes and allowed her thoughts to drift into the realm of possibility.

She saw herself surrounded by books, each one filled with stories and wisdom. It was a dream of knowledge and learning, a reflection of her passion for understanding the mysteries of existence.

She saw herself standing on a stage, speaking to a vast audience. It was a dream of sharing wisdom and inspiration, a reflection of her desire to uplift and empower others.

She saw herself in a peaceful garden, surrounded by flowers and flowing water. It was a dream of serenity and healing, a reflection of her longing for inner peace and harmony.

Elias watched as Sarah's dreams and aspirations took shape in the realm, her thoughts and intentions manifesting into vibrant scenes and experiences. "The Realm of Dreams is a place where your dreams and aspirations come to life, Sarah. It is a reminder that your thoughts and intentions hold the power to shape your reality."

As Sarah continued to explore her dreams and aspirations in the realm, she encountered a series of portals that seemed to lead to different aspects of her own consciousness. Each portal held the promise of self-discovery and transformation.

The first portal led to a chamber filled with mirrors that reflected her past experiences and choices. She saw moments of joy and moments of challenge, moments of growth and moments of introspection. It was a journey through the tapestry of her own life, a reflection of the choices that had brought her to this moment.

The second portal revealed a chamber adorned with paintings and murals that depicted her present experiences and relationships. She saw herself surrounded by friends and loved ones, each one playing a unique role in her journey. It was a visual narrative of her current existence, a reflection of the connections that enriched her life.

The third portal opened into a chamber filled with the soothing sound of flowing water. In the center of the chamber was a tranquil pool, much like the one at the entrance of the temple. But this pool was special—it held reflections of her future dreams and aspirations. Sarah gazed into the pool, seeing images of her own potential and the path that lay before her. It was a reminder that her journey was a continuous evolution toward her highest self.

The fourth portal revealed a chamber illuminated by a soft, radiant light. In the center of the room was a luminous crystal that seemed to pulse with energy. Sarah approached the crystal and placed her hand upon it. She felt a surge of insight and intuition flow through her. It was a chamber of inner wisdom and guidance, a reminder that her inner voice was a powerful compass on her journey.

Elias watched as Sarah explored the chambers of self-discovery and transformation with a sense of courage and introspection. "The Realm of Dreams challenges you to explore the multi-dimensional aspects of your own consciousness, Sarah. It is a place of empowerment and self-awareness."

Chapter 16: The Path of Integration

After their profound experiences in the Realm of Dreams, Sarah and Elias embarked on the next leg of their journey through the afterlife. Their path led them to a place known as the Path of Integration.

This path was unlike any they had encountered before. It stretched out before them, weaving through a landscape of ever-changing colors and forms. It was as if they were walking through the very fabric of existence, where all aspects of consciousness converged and merged.

Elias spoke with a sense of reverence, "Welcome to the Path of Integration, Sarah. This is a place where the fragmented aspects of the self come together, where the threads of experience and knowledge unite to form a greater whole."

Sarah looked around in wonder, trying to make sense of the swirling colors and forms that surrounded her. It was as if she had entered a realm where past, present, and future existed simultaneously, where all the experiences and knowledge she had gained in her journey converged.

"What will we find here?" she asked, her voice filled with curiosity.

Elias smiled, his presence a source of guidance and support. "In the Path of Integration, you can merge your past, present, and future experiences into a harmonious whole. It is a place of self-discovery and synthesis."

As they ventured deeper into the path, Sarah began to notice that the colors and forms around her represented different aspects of her own consciousness. She saw vibrant hues of joy and laughter, swirling patterns of curiosity and wonder, and deep, tranquil pools of introspection and contemplation.

Elias explained, "In the Path of Integration, the fragmented aspects of the self are brought together into a unified whole, Sarah. It is a reminder that your journey is not just a series of separate experiences but a tapestry of interconnected wisdom."

Sarah marveled at the idea that all her experiences and

knowledge were interwoven into a greater tapestry of understanding. It was a testament to the richness of her journey and the interconnectedness of all existence.

As they continued to walk along the path, Sarah began to feel a sense of resonance with the different aspects of her consciousness. She noticed that her thoughts and emotions began to merge and harmonize, creating a sense of inner peace and unity.

Elias watched with pride as Sarah began to integrate the fragmented aspects of her own consciousness. "The Path of Integration allows you to harmonize your inner experiences and knowledge, Sarah. It is a place of inner balance and synthesis."

With newfound clarity and self-awareness, Sarah realized that the path also offered her the opportunity to integrate her past, present, and future experiences. She closed her eyes and allowed her thoughts to drift into the realm of possibility.

She saw herself as a child, full of innocence and curiosity, exploring the wonders of the world with wide-eyed wonder. She felt a sense of connection to her younger self, recognizing that the essence of who she was had always been a part of her.

She saw herself in the present moment, navigating the complexities of life with grace and resilience. She felt a deep sense of acceptance for her current self, recognizing that every choice and experience had led her to this point.

She saw herself in the future, standing on the threshold of new adventures and possibilities. She felt a sense of anticipation and excitement for the person she was becoming, recognizing that the future was a canvas waiting to be painted.

Elias spoke with a sense of affirmation, "The Path of Integration allows you to merge your past, present, and future into a seamless tapestry of experience, Sarah. It is a reminder that your journey is a continuous evolution of consciousness."

As they journeyed further along the path, Sarah encountered a series of portals that seemed to lead to different aspects of her own consciousness. Each portal held the promise of self-discovery and transformation.

The first portal led to a chamber filled with mirrors that reflected her past experiences and choices. She saw moments of joy and moments of challenge, moments of growth and moments of introspection. It was a journey through the tapestry of her own life, a reflection of the choices that had brought her to this moment.

The second portal revealed a chamber adorned with paintings and murals that depicted her present experiences and relationships. She saw herself surrounded by friends and loved ones, each one playing a unique role in her journey. It was a visual narrative of her current existence, a reflection of the connections that enriched her life.

The third portal opened into a chamber filled with the soothing sound of flowing water. In the center of the chamber was a tranquil pool, much like the one at the entrance of the temple. But this pool was special—it held reflections of her future dreams and aspirations. Sarah gazed into the pool, seeing images of her own potential and the path that lay before her. It was a reminder that her journey was a continuous evolution toward her highest self.

The fourth portal revealed a chamber illuminated by a

soft, radiant light. In the center of the room was a luminous crystal that seemed to pulse with energy. Sarah approached the crystal and placed her hand upon it. She felt a surge of insight and intuition flow through her. It was a chamber of inner wisdom and guidance, a reminder that her inner voice was a powerful compass on her journey.

Elias watched as Sarah explored the chambers of self-discovery and transformation with a sense of courage and introspection. "The Path of Integration challenges you to harmonize your inner experiences and knowledge, Sarah. It is a place of empowerment and self-awareness."

As Sarah emerged from the deepest chambers of the path, she felt a profound sense of transformation and renewal. She had integrated the fragmented aspects of her own consciousness, harmonizing her past, present, and future experiences into a seamless tapestry of understanding. She understood that her journey in the afterlife was a continuous evolution of consciousness and self-discovery.

One evening, as she sat in quiet contemplation along the path, she felt a presence beside her—a presence that emanated a profound sense of unity and completeness. It was the guardian of the path, their luminous form radiating a sense of fulfillment.

The guardian spoke with a voice that resonated with wisdom and love. "You have journeyed deep within the chambers of your own consciousness, Sarah. You have integrated the fragmented aspects of your self and embraced the unity of your experiences. It is time to carry this wisdom and transformation forward on your journey."

Sarah nodded in gratitude, her heart filled with a deep sense of fulfillment. She knew that her journey in the afterlife was a testament to the power of self-discovery and the continuous exploration of consciousness.

With a sense of purpose and unity, she left the Path of Integration behind, carrying with her a renewed understanding of her own consciousness and the interconnectedness of all existence.

And so, as Sarah and Elias continued their journey through the afterlife, they knew that the mysteries of existence continued to beckon. The path had been a place of profound self-discovery and transformation, a reminder that the soul's journey was a continuous evolution of consciousness and growth.

Chapter 17: The Symphony of Souls

As Sarah and Elias continued their journey through the afterlife, they found themselves in a realm that resonated with a profound sense of harmony and unity—the Symphony of Souls.

This realm was unlike any they had encountered before. It was a vast expanse of vibrant energy and light, where every soul that had ever existed was represented as a unique musical note. These notes blended together in a harmonious symphony that filled the air with a melodious and transcendent sound.

Elias spoke with a sense of awe, "Welcome to the Symphony of Souls, Sarah. This is a place where the collective consciousness of all existence is expressed as a symphony of harmony and unity."

Sarah stood still, her senses overwhelmed by the beauty and serenity of the symphony. It was as if the very essence of existence was resonating in perfect harmony, creating a tapestry of interconnectedness.

"What is this place?" she asked in hushed wonder.

Elias smiled, his presence a source of reassurance and guidance. "In the Symphony of Souls, you can experience the interconnectedness of all existence, gain insights into the collective wisdom of souls, and join in the creation of a harmonious whole."

As they ventured deeper into the realm, Sarah realized that the notes of the symphony were not just abstract sounds but representations of individual souls. Each note carried a unique frequency and vibration, and together, they created a symphony that transcended time and space.

She noticed that the symphony was not just a passive creation but an active and evolving expression of the souls that composed it. Souls flowed through the symphony, merging and harmonizing their energies in an ever-changing dance of unity.

Elias explained, "In the Symphony of Souls, you can connect with the energies and intentions of all souls, Sarah. It is a place of unity and shared expression."

As they continued to explore, Sarah felt a sense of resonance with the symphony. She realized that her own energy and essence were a part of this harmonious whole, contributing to the collective tapestry of existence.

She extended her senses further and began to hear the melodies of individual souls. She heard the notes of joy and laughter, the notes of sorrow and healing, and the notes of wisdom and inspiration. It was as if the souls were speaking to her through their unique frequencies.

Elias watched with a sense of pride as Sarah began to attune herself to the symphony. "The Symphony of Souls allows you to listen to the voices and intentions of all souls, Sarah. It is a place of deep connection and shared wisdom."

With newfound understanding, Sarah realized that the symphony also offered her the opportunity to contribute her own unique note to the collective harmony. She closed her eyes and allowed her own energy and intention to flow into the symphony.

She felt her note merge with the others, creating a beautiful and harmonious chord that resonated with love and unity. It was a reminder that her presence in the afterlife was not just about receiving but also about giving, about contributing to the greater symphony of existence.

Elias spoke with a sense of affirmation, "The Symphony of Souls allows you to express your own unique energy and intention, Sarah. It is a place of co-creation and shared expression."

As they journeyed further into the realm, Sarah realized that the symphony also had the power to reflect the experiences and intentions of all souls. She noticed that the melodies of the symphony shifted and changed, responding to the thoughts and emotions of the souls that composed it.

She witnessed moments of joy and celebration, where the symphony soared with exuberant melodies. She witnessed moments of introspection and contemplation, where the symphony took on a serene and meditative quality. It was a reflection of the collective consciousness and the ever-changing nature of existence.

Elias explained, "The Symphony of Souls is a mirror of the experiences and intentions of all souls, Sarah. It is a reminder that your thoughts and emotions have the power to shape your reality."

With this realization, Sarah became more attuned to her own thoughts and intentions, understanding that they had a direct impact on the symphony and the collective consciousness. She began to channel her intentions toward love, harmony, and unity, knowing that her energy contributed to the greater whole.

As they continued to explore, Sarah noticed that the symphony had a transformative power. It had the ability to heal and uplift the souls that experienced it. She witnessed souls who had carried burdens of sorrow and pain being enveloped by the healing melodies of the symphony, their energies transforming into states of peace and serenity.

Elias watched with a sense of compassion as Sarah witnessed these moments of transformation. "The Symphony of Souls has the power to heal and uplift, Sarah. It is a place of profound healing and transformation."

With a sense of purpose, Sarah began to channel her intentions toward healing and transformation, extending her energy to those souls who sought solace and renewal in the symphony. She felt a deep sense of connection and compassion for all the souls she encountered.

One evening, as she sat in quiet contemplation within

the symphony, she felt a presence beside her—a presence that emanated a profound sense of love and guidance. She turned to see a luminous figure,

Chapter 18: The Heart of Understanding

The luminous figure who had appeared beside Sarah in the Symphony of Souls radiated a warm and comforting presence. It was as if a gentle light enveloped them, illuminating the space around them.

The figure spoke with a voice that resonated with wisdom and love. "I am a guardian of the Symphony of Souls, Sarah. I am here to assist you on your journey of connection and understanding."

Sarah felt an immediate sense of trust and connection with the guardian. She knew that this encounter was not a mere coincidence but a profound moment of guidance and support.

With a sense of humility, she asked, "What wisdom do you have to share with me?"

The guardian smiled, their presence filling the symphony with a deep sense of peace. "In the Symphony of Souls, you have witnessed the interconnectedness of all existence, the power of shared intention, and the transformative nature of harmony. It is a reflection of the unity that underlies all creation."

Sarah nodded, her heart filled with a sense of understanding. She had experienced the symphony as a place of connection and unity, a reminder that all souls were part of a greater whole.

The guardian continued, "But there is a deeper layer of

understanding that the symphony can offer, Sarah. It is the understanding of the heart, the recognition that love is the essence of all existence."

Sarah listened intently, her curiosity piqued. She had journeyed through realms of knowledge and wisdom, and now she was ready to explore the profound wisdom of the heart.

The guardian spoke with a gentle assurance, "The heart is the seat of love and compassion, the source of empathy and understanding. In the Symphony of Souls, you have the opportunity to connect with the heart of all souls, to experience the depth of love that unites all existence."

With the guardian as her guide, Sarah closed her eyes and allowed her awareness to shift from the melodies of the symphony to the heartbeats of the souls that composed it. She felt a subtle shift in her perception, as if she was attuning herself to the very essence of existence.

She heard the heartbeats of souls pulsating with love and compassion, each one like a radiant star in the symphony. She heard the heartbeats of souls seeking healing and understanding, their energies calling out for love and solace.

Elias watched with a sense of pride as Sarah connected with the heartbeats of the souls in the symphony. "The heart is the gateway to understanding and compassion, Sarah. It is a place of profound connection and empathy."

As she continued to attune herself to the heartbeats, Sarah noticed that each heartbeat carried a unique signature, a resonance that was as individual as the soul it represented. Yet, beneath this individuality, there was a common thread of love that united them all.

The guardian spoke softly, "In the heart of understanding, you can connect with the essence of love that unites all souls, Sarah. It is a reminder that love is the universal language of the soul."

Sarah felt a deep sense of gratitude for the opportunity to connect with the heartbeats of the souls in the symphony. It was a profound experience of unity and empathy, a recognition that love was the unifying force that transcended all differences.

With the guardian's guidance, she extended her own heart energy to the souls in the symphony, offering love and compassion to those who sought healing and understanding. She felt her own heart expand with each act of love, knowing that her intentions were contributing to the greater harmony of the symphony.

Elias spoke with a sense of affirmation, "The heart of understanding allows you to express your own love and compassion, Sarah. It is a place of shared empathy and healing."

As they continued to explore the heart of understanding, Sarah realized that it also held the power to heal and transform her own consciousness. She felt her own heart energy being uplifted and purified, as if the very act of giving love and compassion was a source of inner renewal.

The guardian explained, "In the heart of understanding, you not only connect with the essence of love in all souls but also experience the healing and transformation of your own heart, Sarah. It is a place of deep inner renewal."

With this realization, Sarah allowed her own heart to be transformed by the love and compassion she extended to others. She felt a deep sense of inner peace and fulfillment, a recognition that love was the key to her own evolution of consciousness.

One evening, as she sat in quiet contemplation within the heart of understanding, she felt a presence beside her—a presence that emanated a profound sense of love and unity. She turned to see the luminous figure, the guardian of the Symphony of Souls, standing beside her.

The guardian spoke with a voice filled with love and wisdom. "You have journeyed to the heart of understanding, Sarah, and in doing so, you have experienced the depth of love that unites all souls. It is a reminder that love is the essence of all existence."

Sarah nodded, her heart filled with a sense of profound understanding and connection. She knew that her journey in the afterlife was not just about acquiring knowledge and wisdom but also about experiencing the transformative power of love.

The guardian continued, "As you carry this wisdom of the heart with you, remember that love is the universal language of the soul, the bridge that unites all differences. It is a reminder that every soul, no matter how unique, is connected by the thread of love."

With a sense of gratitude and love, Sarah left the Symphony of Souls behind, carrying with her the wisdom of the heart and the recognition that love was the essence of all existence.

And so, as Sarah and Elias continued their journey through the afterlife, they knew that the mysteries of existence continued to beckon. The heart of understanding had been a place of profound connection and compassion, a reminder that love was the universal language of the soul.

**"Beyond the Veil:
Journeys in the Afterlife"
By
Doug Hensley**

Chapter 1: The Protagonist's Death

Chapter 2: Awakening in the Afterlife

Chapter 3: The Welcome Committee

Chapter 4: Revisiting Life Memories

Chapter 5: The Soul's Journey

Chapter 6: Meeting Lost Loved Ones

Chapter 7: The Library of Life

Chapter 8: Lessons from the Past

Chapter 9: The Council of Elders

Chapter 10: The Bridge Between Worlds

Chapter 11: The Shadow Realm

Chapter 12: Love in the Afterlife

Chapter 13: The Great Beyond

Chapter 14: A Second Chance

Chapter 15: The River of Time

Chapter 16: The Final Judgment

Chapter 17: Farewell to the Afterlife

Chapter 18: The Reincarnation

Author's Notes

"In a realm beyond life as we know it, Sarah embarks on an extraordinary journey through the afterlife. From the mysterious Temple of Reflection to the ethereal Symphony of Souls, she explores realms of wisdom, unity, and love that challenge the very fabric of existence. As Sarah's quest unfolds, she discovers that the key to her own transformation lies not in knowledge alone, but in the boundless power of love and compassion. Join her on this riveting odyssey of the soul, where the mysteries of the afterlife come alive, and the heart reveals the true essence of existence."

Chapter 1: The Protagonist's Death

The night was cold and drizzling, a fitting backdrop to the tragic events that were about to unfold. Sarah, our protagonist, had never paid much attention to the weather, but that night, it seemed like even the heavens were mourning. She was driving along a winding road, her hands gripping the steering wheel with white-knuckled intensity. Her heart raced, not just from the rain-slicked roads, but from the argument she'd had with her best friend, Mark, just moments ago.

The argument had been explosive, a culmination of months of tension and misunderstandings. Sarah had wanted to make amends, to set things right between them, but Mark had been adamant, his anger unyielding. He had slammed the door of their shared apartment, leaving Sarah in a cloud of frustration and hurt.

As the headlights of her car cut through the darkness, Sarah's thoughts were in turmoil. She wished she could turn back time, erase the bitter words exchanged between them, and tell Mark how much he meant to her. But it was too late for that now.

Her phone buzzed, a message notification that she instinctively reached for. It was a text from Mark, a simple "I'm sorry" followed by a heart emoji. Tears blurred her vision as she read it. She was about to reply when the sound of screeching tires and blaring horns shattered the night.

Sarah's car swerved out of control, a sickening sensation of weightlessness engulfing her as it veered off the road. Time seemed to slow as her car tumbled down an embankment, the world spinning in a dizzying whirl of lights and sounds. She caught glimpses of trees, rain-slicked leaves, and the dark expanse of the night sky.

Then, there was a deafening crash, and everything went black.

When Sarah regained consciousness, it wasn't the blinding white light she had heard about in stories of near-death experiences. Instead, she found herself in a place that felt strangely familiar, yet entirely different. It was as if she had stepped into a dreamscape, a world of ethereal beauty.

She was standing in a meadow bathed in a soft, silvery light. The grass beneath her feet was impossibly lush and vibrant, and the air carried a scent of blooming flowers and earthy freshness. The sky above was a mesmerizing blend of colors that shifted and changed like a living canvas. It was a place of breathtaking beauty, unlike anything she had ever seen.

Confusion gripped Sarah. She touched her body, half-expecting to find herself injured or in pain, but she felt nothing. She was whole, unharmed, and wearing the same clothes she had on before the accident.

"Where am I?" she whispered to herself, her voice barely more than a breath of wind.

As if in answer to her question, a figure began to materialize before her. It was a woman, radiant and graceful, with eyes that seemed to hold the wisdom of ages. She wore a flowing gown that shimmered like liquid silver, and her presence exuded a sense of profound serenity.

"Welcome, Sarah," the woman said, her voice a melodic blend of warmth and reassurance. "You have crossed over to the other side, to the realm beyond life as you know it."

Sarah's heart raced as she tried to make sense of it all. "Am I... am I dead?"

The woman nodded gently. "Yes, but fear not, for this is not the end. It is a new beginning."

Tears welled up in Sarah's eyes as the weight of her own mortality settled upon her. She had so many questions, so many uncertainties about what lay ahead. But one thing was clear: her journey in the afterlife had just begun.

And so, in that surreal meadow bathed in silver light, Sarah took her first step into the unknown, leaving behind the world she knew for a realm where the mysteries of life and death would unfold in ways she could never have imagined.

This extended version of Chapter 1 sets the stage for Sarah's journey in the afterlife and introduces the mysterious woman who will guide her. You can continue to develop the story, exploring Sarah's emotions, her interactions in this new realm, and the mysteries that lie ahead in subsequent chapters.

Chapter 2: Awakening in the Afterlife

Sarah stood in the meadow, her eyes fixed on the enigmatic woman who had welcomed her to this otherworldly realm. The woman's presence exuded a sense of peace and understanding that washed over Sarah like a soothing balm.

"I know this is overwhelming," the woman said, her voice a comforting melody. "But you are safe here, Sarah."

Sarah nodded, her thoughts a whirlwind of confusion and wonder. She took in her surroundings once more, noticing the subtle details that made this place unlike anything she had ever experienced. The grass beneath her feet seemed to emit a soft, melodic hum, as if it were alive. Flowers of every hue danced in the gentle breeze, their petals emitting a gentle glow.

As she continued to survey her surroundings, Sarah realized that there were others in the meadow with her. Souls, like herself, who had crossed over from the world of the living. Some were sitting in small groups, engaged in hushed conversations, while others wandered alone, lost in thought.

The woman gestured toward the souls in the meadow. "These are your fellow travelers, Sarah. Souls from all walks of life, each with their own unique journey."

Sarah watched in awe as the souls moved about, their forms radiant and translucent, like faintly glowing stars. She couldn't help but wonder about the stories hidden within each one, the experiences that had led them to this place.

The woman extended a hand toward Sarah. "Come, let me show you more of this realm."

With a sense of curiosity and a trace of trepidation, Sarah took the woman's hand. They began to walk through the meadow, and as they did, Sarah noticed that the silvery light surrounding them seemed to respond to their presence, creating intricate patterns in the air.

"What is this place?" Sarah finally managed to ask.

The woman smiled gently. "This is a place of transition, a realm between the world of the living and what lies beyond. Some call it the Threshold. Here, souls like yours find solace, healing, and guidance before continuing their journey."

Sarah absorbed the words, trying to make sense of her new reality. "But what happens next? Where do we go from here?"

The woman's eyes held a hint of mystery. "That, my dear, depends on the choices you make, the lessons you learn, and the path you follow. The afterlife is vast and full of possibilities."

As they walked, they came upon a tranquil pond, its surface as smooth as glass. Sarah could see her reflection, but it was not the reflection of the person she had been in life. It was a reflection of her true essence, her soul, free from the constraints of her earthly form.

"Who am I now?" Sarah whispered, her voice trembling.

The woman's gaze remained fixed on the pond. "You are who you have always been, Sarah. You are a soul, a being of light and energy, bound by neither time nor space. In this realm, you are your truest self."

Sarah felt a mixture of awe and acceptance wash over her. She had spent her life searching for meaning, for a sense of purpose. Now, in this otherworldly place, she had the opportunity to discover who she truly was.

As they continued their journey, Sarah couldn't help but

think of the world she had left behind—the people she loved, the dreams she had pursued, and the mistakes she had made. It was a bittersweet reflection, a reminder of the complexity of her human existence.

The woman turned to her, her eyes filled with compassion. "You carry the memories of your earthly life with you, Sarah. They are a part of your journey, a part of what makes you who you are."

Tears welled up in Sarah's eyes as she thought of the people she had lost, the moments of joy and sorrow that had shaped her. She wasn't sure what lay ahead in this afterlife, but one thing was certain: it was a place of profound transformation and discovery.

And so, in that tranquil meadow, surrounded by the radiant souls of fellow travelers, Sarah began to embrace the mysteries of the afterlife, ready to embark on a journey that would challenge her, heal her, and ultimately lead her to the answers she sought.

Chapter 3: The Welcome Committee

As Sarah walked alongside the radiant woman through the tranquil meadow, she couldn't help but feel a sense of peace and wonder settling within her. The meadow stretched on, seemingly endless, but each step she took was a step further into the mysteries of the afterlife.

As they walked, the woman began to explain more about this realm. "Many souls arrive here in various states of confusion and uncertainty. That's where we come in, those of us who have been here for some time. We help newcomers like you acclimate to this new existence."

Sarah nodded, grateful for the guidance. "How long have you been here?"

The woman's smile held a touch of ancient wisdom. "Time is different in this place, Sarah. It's not measured as it is in the world of the living. I've been here for what you might perceive as a long time, but it feels both eternal and fleeting."

As they continued to walk, Sarah noticed figures approaching in the distance. They were other beings like the woman, their forms shimmering with a gentle radiance. They gathered around, forming a welcoming committee of sorts. Each one had a unique presence, and their eyes held a depth of understanding that seemed to reach into the very essence of Sarah's being.

One of the beings, a man with a serene countenance, stepped forward. "Welcome, Sarah. I am Elias. We are here to assist you on your journey through the afterlife."

Sarah extended her hand to shake his, but to her surprise, their hands passed through each other as if they were made of mist. She withdrew her hand, momentarily taken aback.

Elias chuckled warmly. "In this realm, physical touch is not necessary. We communicate on a different level, one that transcends the limitations of the physical world."

Sarah nodded, still trying to grasp the nature of this existence. "I have so many questions. What is this place, and what comes next?"

Elias gestured toward the meadow and the souls who moved about. "This is a place of transition, a realm where souls find healing, reflection, and guidance. What comes next is a journey unique to each soul. Some choose to move on to higher realms, while others may opt for reincarnation."

Sarah's mind buzzed with curiosity. "Reincarnation? You mean I could come back to life?"

Elias nodded. "Yes, if you choose to do so. Reincarnation is an opportunity for further growth and learning. It allows your soul to experience different aspects of existence."

The thought of returning to the world of the living filled Sarah with a mix of excitement and trepidation. She had so many unresolved questions, unfulfilled dreams, and relationships she wished she could mend. The idea of a second chance was tantalizing.

Another being, a woman with luminous eyes, stepped forward. "But that decision is not one to be made hastily, Sarah. Your experiences in this realm will help you understand the implications of your choices."

Sarah nodded, realizing that she had much to learn about the afterlife and herself. She looked around at the welcoming committee, a group of souls who had undoubtedly faced their own trials and tribulations in their journeys.

"What should I do now?" she asked.

Elias spoke with a gentle tone. "First, take your time to explore this place, to reflect on your life, and to seek understanding. You'll have opportunities to revisit your memories and learn from your experiences. We'll be here to guide you every step of the way."

And so, Sarah embarked on her journey in the afterlife, surrounded by the radiant beings of the welcome committee and the enigmatic woman who had greeted her. The meadow was just the beginning, a place of healing and transformation where her true exploration of the afterlife would unfold.

In this extended Chapter 3, Sarah encounters the welcoming committee of beings who help newcomers like her adjust to the afterlife. They provide her with information about the nature of this realm and the choices that lie ahead. Sarah's journey of self-discovery and understanding begins to take shape, and she realizes that the afterlife holds many secrets and opportunities for growth.

Chapter 4: Revisiting Life Memories

In the days that followed her arrival in the afterlife, Sarah found herself drawn to a unique place within the ethereal realm—an expansive garden where the boundaries of time and memory seemed to blur. This garden held the key to one of the most profound experiences in the afterlife—the opportunity to revisit the memories of her life.

Guided by the luminous beings who had welcomed her, Sarah entered the garden. The air was filled with the scent of blossoms, and the soft music of nature's orchestra played in the background, creating an atmosphere of serenity. The path she walked upon was paved with iridescent stones that seemed to respond to her presence, illuminating her way.

The first memory that came to her was of her childhood home. As she stepped onto a cobblestone pathway, the scene around her transformed. She found herself standing in front of the familiar house where she had spent her early years. The sound of children's laughter filled the air, and she saw her younger self playing in the front yard.

Tears welled up in her eyes as she watched herself, a

carefree child with dreams and innocence. She could feel the warmth of her mother's embrace and the reassuring presence of her father. It was a time of wonder and simplicity, a time when life's complexities had not yet cast their shadow.

The luminous beings who accompanied her watched with understanding. Elias spoke softly, "These memories hold the essence of who you are, Sarah. They are the threads that weave the tapestry of your soul."

As the scene shifted to her teenage years, Sarah saw herself again, filled with the hopes and dreams of adolescence. She remembered the joy of her first crush, the thrill of late-night conversations with friends, and the taste of freedom as she ventured into the world on her own.

But there were also moments of pain and heartache, like the memory of a broken friendship that had haunted her for years. She had always wished she could go back and make amends, and now, in this place, she felt the weight of those unspoken apologies.

The luminous woman who had first greeted her placed a hand on her shoulder. "You have the power to heal old wounds here, to understand the choices you made and the impact they had on others."

Sarah nodded, realizing that this garden of memories was not just a place of reflection but also a place of healing and growth. She watched as the scenes of her life continued to unfold, from the highs of love and achievement to the lows of loss and disappointment.

One memory, in particular, stood out—the day she had stood up to defend a classmate who was being bullied. It was a moment of courage she had almost forgotten, buried beneath the weight of other memories. She saw the grateful smile on her classmate's face, a smile that held the promise of friendship and acceptance.

Elias spoke again, his voice gentle. "These memories are the building blocks of your soul's evolution, Sarah. They are the lessons that shape your path in the afterlife."

As Sarah continued to explore her life's memories, she began to understand the intricate tapestry of her existence. Each moment, whether joyful or painful, had played a role in shaping the person she had become. She realized that her journey in the afterlife was not just about moving forward but also about reconciling with her past.

In the garden of memories, Sarah found solace and clarity. She revisited the moments of love, forgiveness, and growth, and she acknowledged the moments of pain, regret, and missed opportunities. It was a profound journey of self-discovery, a journey that would prepare her for the choices and challenges that lay ahead in the afterlife.

And so, as the memories of her life continued to unfold in the garden, Sarah embraced the lessons they held, knowing that they were the threads that would guide her on her path of transformation in the afterlife.

This extended Chapter 4 delves deeper into Sarah's exploration of her life's memories and the profound lessons they hold. It highlights the healing and growth that can occur in the afterlife as she comes to terms with the complexities of her past. The garden of memories becomes a pivotal setting for her journey of self-discovery.

Chapter 5: The Soul's Journey

In the days that followed Sarah's exploration of the garden of memories, she found herself drawn to another aspect of the afterlife—a realm where souls embarked on journeys of self-discovery and transformation. This realm was a place of exploration and growth, where each soul had the opportunity to understand the depths of their being.

Guided by Elias, the serene being who had become her mentor of sorts, Sarah entered the realm of the soul's journey. It was a vast and ever-changing landscape, filled with landscapes that defied earthly description. Mountains of crystal and rivers of liquid light stretched out before her.

Elias gestured to the breathtaking panorama. "This is where you'll come to understand the nature of your soul, Sarah. Here, you'll embark on a journey of self-discovery and exploration."

Sarah felt a mixture of awe and anticipation as she took in her surroundings. The air was charged with an energy that seemed to pulse with life. She could sense the presence of other souls moving about, each on their unique journeys of understanding.

Her first destination was a crystalline mountain that beckoned to her with an irresistible allure. As she climbed its radiant slopes, she felt a sense of exhilaration and clarity wash over her. The mountain was not just a physical place but a reflection of her inner self, a representation of her aspirations and dreams.

At the summit, Sarah was met by the luminous woman who had first welcomed her to the afterlife. "This mountain is a mirror of your soul's highest aspirations, Sarah. What do you see?"

Sarah gazed out at the breathtaking vista below, a panorama that seemed to stretch on forever. She saw images of the dreams she had once held—the desire to create art, the longing for deep connections, and the quest for knowledge. But she also saw the dreams she had yet to fulfill, the potential waiting to be unlocked.

With newfound clarity, she understood that her journey in the afterlife was not just about reflecting on the past but also about envisioning the future. She felt a renewed sense of purpose, a commitment to pursue her soul's deepest desires.

Elias appeared beside her, his presence a source of guidance and support. "Your journey is a continuous cycle of growth, Sarah. Each step leads to greater self-awareness and understanding."

The next destination on her journey led her to a river of liquid light, where she witnessed scenes from her life replayed in shimmering patterns on the water's surface. It was a river of reflection, a place where she could gain insights into the choices she had made and their impact on her journey.

She watched moments of kindness and compassion, moments of strength and resilience. But she also witnessed moments of doubt and hesitation, moments when fear had held her back. It was a sobering experience, a reminder of the complexities of her humanity.

As she continued her journey, Sarah encountered other souls who shared their stories and insights. She learned about the diverse paths and experiences that had brought them to this realm. Each encounter was a reminder of the interconnectedness of all souls, a web of experiences and lessons that spanned across time and space.

One particularly profound encounter was with a soul who had chosen the path of forgiveness and reconciliation. This soul had experienced great pain and betrayal in life but had found the strength to forgive and heal. The encounter left Sarah with a deep sense of inspiration and the realization that forgiveness was a powerful force that could transform not only individuals but also the world.

As days turned into weeks in the realm of the soul's journey, Sarah's understanding of herself and the afterlife deepened. She began to see her journey not as a linear progression but as a series of interconnected experiences and lessons. Each step was a building block in her soul's evolution, a step closer to realizing her true potential.

And so, in the ever-changing landscape of the afterlife, Sarah embraced the soul's journey with open arms. She knew that the path ahead was filled with challenges and revelations, but she was determined to explore the depths of her being and discover the true essence of her soul.

This extended Chapter 5 delves deeper into Sarah's exploration of the afterlife, specifically the realm of the soul's journey. It explores the transformative experiences and encounters she has along the way and highlights the interconnectedness of souls in this realm. Sarah's journey of self-discovery and growth continues to unfold, shaping her understanding of the afterlife and her place within it.

Chapter 6: Meeting Lost Loved Ones

In the luminous world of the afterlife, Sarah's journey of self-discovery continued to unfold, revealing new facets of her existence with each passing day. Yet, among the countless revelations and encounters, one held a unique place in her heart—the opportunity to reunite with her lost loved ones.

Guided by Elias, the serene being who had become her mentor and guide, Sarah embarked on a journey to reconnect with those who had passed on before her. The thought of seeing her departed family and friends filled her with a mixture of anticipation and emotion. She wondered if they had found peace and happiness in this ethereal realm.

As they walked together through a radiant forest, Elias spoke softly, "The bonds of love and connection are not broken by death, Sarah. They continue to exist in this realm, where the essence of each soul endures."

Sarah's heart swelled with hope as they approached a clearing within the forest. There, in a soft and golden light, she saw familiar faces waiting for her. Her parents, her grandparents, and friends who had departed before her stood with open arms, their smiles radiant with love.

Tears of joy streamed down Sarah's cheeks as she rushed toward them. The sense of reunion was overwhelming as she embraced her parents, feeling the warmth and love that transcended the boundaries of earthly existence.

Her mother, her voice filled with love, spoke softly, "Welcome, dear. We've been waiting for you."

Sarah looked around at the familiar faces, each person representing a cherished memory from her life. Her grandfather, who had taught her the joy of storytelling, shared a tale of an ancient adventure, and her childhood friend reminisced about their adventures in a secret hideaway.

As the hours passed, Sarah laughed and cried, shared stories and memories, and felt the profound sense of belonging that had eluded her in the world of the living. The barriers of time and distance dissolved, and she realized that this realm allowed for a depth of connection that was beyond her wildest dreams.

Her father, with a twinkle in his eye, said, "We've been watching over you, Sarah. We've seen your struggles and your triumphs. We've shared your joys and sorrows."

The realization that her loved ones had been with her, even in her darkest moments, brought a sense of comfort and reassurance. She felt their unconditional love and support in a way she had never imagined possible.

Elias, who had watched the reunion with a serene smile, approached her. "The bonds you share with your loved ones are eternal, Sarah. They are a source of strength and guidance on your journey in the afterlife."

Over the following days, Sarah continued to spend time with her departed loved ones, relishing the moments of connection and shared experiences. Together, they explored the luminous landscapes of the afterlife, embarking on adventures and discoveries that deepened their bonds.

One day, as they walked along the shores of a radiant lake, her grandmother, whose wisdom had always been a source of guidance, shared profound insights about the nature of existence. She spoke of the interconnectedness of all souls, the threads of energy that bound them together, and the endless possibilities of growth and transformation.

Sarah listened with rapt attention, realizing that her journey in the afterlife was not just about personal growth but also about contributing to the collective wisdom and evolution of all souls. The knowledge she gained from her loved ones and her own experiences would become a part of this greater tapestry of understanding.

As time flowed differently in the afterlife, Sarah cherished each moment with her loved ones, knowing that their reunion was not bound by the constraints of earthly time. She understood that this realm offered her the chance to deepen her connections, heal old wounds, and continue to learn from the wisdom of those who had gone before her.

And so, in the luminous world of the afterlife, Sarah's journey took on new dimensions as she reveled in the joy of reuniting with her lost loved ones. The bonds of love and connection that had transcended death became a source of strength and inspiration, guiding her on her path of self-discovery and growth.

This extended Chapter 6 delves deeper into Sarah's emotional reunion with her lost loved ones in the afterlife, highlighting the enduring nature of their connections and the wisdom they share. It explores the transformative impact of these reunions on Sarah's understanding of herself and her place in this ethereal realm.

Chapter 7: The Library of Life

As Sarah's journey through the afterlife continued, she discovered that this ethereal realm held more wonders than she could have ever imagined. One of the most remarkable places she encountered was the Library of Life—a place where the stories and experiences of every soul in existence were recorded.

Guided by Elias, her trusted mentor and companion, Sarah entered the library with a sense of reverence. The moment she stepped through its shimmering doors, she was enveloped in an atmosphere of wisdom and knowledge. The library stretched out endlessly in all directions, with towering shelves filled with bound volumes, each emanating a soft, radiant light.

Elias spoke, his voice filled with awe, "This is the repository of all existence, Sarah. Every soul's journey, every thought, every emotion, is recorded here."

Sarah's eyes widened in wonder as she gazed at the vastness of the library. "But how can everything be contained in this place?"

Elias smiled, a knowing glint in his eyes. "In the afterlife, space and time are not bound by the same limitations as in the world of the living. Here, the library exists as a reflection of the collective consciousness of all souls."

As they ventured deeper into the library, Sarah began to notice the bound volumes taking on a life of their own. They pulsed with energy, and as she reached out to touch one, she found herself immersed in a vivid and immersive experience—a glimpse into the life and experiences of a soul.

She watched a mother's loving embrace as she held her newborn child for the first time, felt the heartache of a soldier bidding farewell to his family before going off to war, and witnessed the exhilaration of an artist creating a masterpiece. Each volume held a unique story, a perspective on life that was both familiar and utterly unique.

One volume caught her attention—a simple leather-bound book that seemed to radiate a gentle warmth. She picked it up, and as she opened it, she found herself transported into her own life's story. She watched her childhood unfold, her dreams and aspirations taking shape, and the moments of triumph and tribulation that had shaped her journey.

Elias watched as Sarah delved into her own story, his expression filled with understanding. "The library not only contains the stories of others but also offers you the opportunity to gain insights into your own journey, to see the tapestry of your existence in its entirety."

Sarah nodded, her heart filled with a profound sense of gratitude. She saw the choices she had made, the paths she had taken, and the moments that had defined her. It was a journey of self-discovery, a chance to understand the significance of her own experiences.

As she continued to explore the library, Sarah encountered other souls who were also navigating the vast repository of knowledge. Some were seeking answers to profound questions, while others were reliving cherished memories or revisiting moments of regret.

One soul, a philosopher who had pondered the mysteries of existence in life, engaged Sarah in a deep conversation about the nature of consciousness and the interconnectedness of all souls. They explored the profound wisdom contained within the library and the idea that every soul's journey contributed to the collective evolution of consciousness.

Elias joined the conversation, adding his insights and guidance. "The library is a place of reflection and illumination, Sarah. It offers you the chance to gain a deeper understanding of the complexities of existence and your role in the grand tapestry of life."

As days turned into weeks within the Library of Life, Sarah's appreciation for the boundless knowledge it contained grew. She realized that this place was not just a repository of stories but also a source of profound wisdom, a reflection of the infinite possibilities of existence.

One day, as she stood before a particularly radiant volume, Elias spoke softly, "The library also holds the stories of those who have yet to be born, the souls waiting to embark on their own journeys. It is a reminder that life is a continuum, a cycle of growth and evolution."

Sarah nodded, her heart filled with a sense of purpose. She understood that her journey in the afterlife was not just about reflecting on the past but also about contributing to the future. The stories she would share, the wisdom she would gain, would become a part of the ever-expanding tapestry of existence.

And so, in the Library of Life, surrounded by the stories and experiences of countless souls, Sarah continued her journey of self-discovery and growth. She explored the mysteries of existence, gained profound insights into the nature of consciousness, and marveled at the boundless possibilities of life.

This extended Chapter 7 delves deeper into Sarah's

exploration of the afterlife, specifically her experience within the Library of Life. It highlights the profound wisdom and insights she gains from this remarkable place, as well as the opportunity to reflect on her own life's journey. The library becomes a symbol of the interconnectedness of all souls and the collective evolution of consciousness.

Chapter 8: The Trial of Self-Reflection

In the luminous world of the afterlife, Sarah's journey of self-discovery and growth continued to lead her to new and profound experiences. One of the most transformative challenges she encountered was the Trial of Self-Reflection—a test of her understanding, empathy, and ability to confront her own inner demons.

Guided by Elias, her trusted mentor, Sarah arrived at a place within the ethereal realm that seemed to shimmer with an otherworldly intensity. It was a place of introspection and revelation, where the boundaries of her own consciousness would be pushed to their limits.

Elias spoke with solemnity, "The Trial of Self-Reflection is a pivotal moment in your journey, Sarah. It will test your understanding of yourself and your capacity for empathy."

Sarah nodded, her heart filled with a mix of anticipation and trepidation. She knew that this trial would challenge her in ways she could not fully comprehend. She took a deep breath and entered the radiant chamber before her.

Inside, she found herself standing before a mirror—an immense, shimmering mirror that seemed to reflect not only her physical form but also the depths of her soul. As she gazed into it, she saw not just her own image but also the images of those she had encountered in her life—the people she had loved, the people she had hurt, and the people she had misunderstood.

Elias stood beside her, his presence a source of comfort and guidance. "The mirror reveals not only your own reflection, Sarah, but also the reflections of the souls you have touched in your journey."

Sarah's heart pounded as she watched the scenes in the mirror unfold. She saw moments of kindness and compassion, moments when she had offered a helping hand or a comforting word. Those images filled her with a sense of pride and warmth.

But there were also moments of pain and regret, moments when her actions had caused harm or when she had failed to understand the struggles of others. The mirror showed her the faces of people she had hurt, the wounds she had inflicted, and the words she wished she could take back.

Tears welled up in Sarah's eyes as she confronted the mistakes and shortcomings of her earthly existence. She saw the hurt in the eyes of a friend she had let down, the disappointment in a family member she had misunderstood, and the pain of a stranger she had ignored.

Elias spoke softly, his voice filled with compassion, "The Trial of Self-Reflection asks you to confront the shadows within yourself, Sarah. It is an opportunity to acknowledge your mistakes, seek forgiveness, and grow from your experiences."

Sarah nodded, her determination to face her own shortcomings unwavering. She knew that this trial was not about self-condemnation but about self-awareness and growth. She watched as the mirror continued to reveal moments from her life, both the moments of light and the moments of darkness.

As she gazed into the mirror, Sarah saw something unexpected—a reflection of herself as a child, innocent and full of wonder. It was a reminder of the pure and unblemished soul that she had once been, the essence of her true self.

With newfound clarity, she understood that the Trial of Self-Reflection was not just about acknowledging her mistakes but also about reclaiming her own innocence and authenticity. It was about reconnecting with the childlike wonder and compassion that had always resided within her.

As the trial continued, Sarah encountered the reflections of people from her past, including those she had lost touch with and those she had longed to reconnect with. The mirror became a portal to moments of forgiveness and reconciliation, as well as an opportunity to express remorse and seek forgiveness.

One reflection, in particular, stood out—a friend she had drifted apart from due to misunderstandings and miscommunications. Sarah watched as the mirror revealed a heartfelt conversation in which they both acknowledged their mistakes and rekindled their friendship. It was a moment of healing and renewal, a reminder that it was never too late to mend broken bonds.

Elias watched with a knowing smile. "The Trial of Self-Reflection is not just a test, Sarah, but also a chance for redemption and growth. It allows you to heal old wounds and forge deeper connections with the souls you have encountered."

As the trial reached its conclusion, Sarah felt a profound sense of transformation within herself. She had confronted her own shadows, acknowledged her mistakes, and sought forgiveness where it was needed. The mirror now reflected not only the complexities of her existence but also the potential for growth and renewal.

Elias placed a hand on her shoulder, his eyes filled with pride. "You have passed the trial, Sarah. You have shown the capacity for self-awareness, empathy, and growth. This experience will continue to shape your journey in the afterlife."

Sarah nodded, her heart filled with a sense of liberation and renewal. She understood that her journey was not just about self-discovery but also about the capacity for growth and transformation that resided within every soul.

And so, as she left the chamber of the Trial of Self-Reflection, Sarah carried with her a deeper understanding of herself and a renewed sense of purpose. The trial had tested her, challenged her, and ultimately allowed her to embrace the light and darkness within her own soul.

This extended Chapter 8 delves deeper into Sarah's challenging experience in the Trial of Self-Reflection within the afterlife. It highlights her introspection,

Chapter 9: The Realm of Transformation

As Sarah's journey through the afterlife continued, she found herself drawn to a realm unlike any she had encountered before—the Realm of Transformation. Guided by Elias, her trusted mentor, she entered a place of profound change and renewal, where the very essence of souls underwent a remarkable metamorphosis.

The realm was a surreal landscape, filled with vibrant colors and surreal landscapes that defied earthly description. It was as if the laws of physics and nature had been rewritten, allowing for endless possibilities of transformation. The air was charged with an electric energy that sent shivers of anticipation down Sarah's spine.

Elias spoke with a sense of reverence, "This is the Realm of Transformation, Sarah. Here, souls undergo a profound metamorphosis, shedding their old selves and emerging anew."

Sarah looked around, her eyes wide with wonder. "What kind of transformation takes place here?"

Elias gestured toward a shimmering pool of liquid light at the center of the realm. "Each soul's transformation is unique, reflecting their own desires, challenges, and aspirations. It is a process of shedding the layers of the past and embracing the potential for growth and renewal."

As Sarah approached the pool, she saw her reflection in the liquid light, but it was not her earthly self she saw—it was a vision of her highest potential, her truest essence. She saw herself as an artist, a healer, a friend, and a seeker of wisdom, all merged into one radiant being.

With a sense of determination, she stepped into the pool, feeling the liquid light envelop her. It was as if every cell in her body was being infused with a new energy, a sense of purpose and possibility. She felt herself shedding the weight of past regrets and limitations, and a profound sense of liberation washed over her.

As she emerged from the pool, she looked at herself with fresh eyes, feeling a deep sense of self-acceptance and love. She had undergone a transformation, not just in her appearance but in her essence. She had tapped into her highest potential, her true self.

Elias nodded with approval. "The Realm of Transformation allows you to connect with your true essence, to shed the limitations and fears that have held you back in life. It is a place of rebirth and renewal."

Over the following days, Sarah continued to explore the realm, witnessing the transformations of other souls. She saw a soul who had lived a life of fear and insecurity emerge as a being of courage and confidence. She saw a soul burdened by past traumas shed their pain and embrace a life of healing and compassion.

Each transformation was a testament to the resilience and potential of the soul, a reminder that growth and renewal were not just possible but inherent to the nature of existence.

One day, as she ventured deeper into the realm, she encountered a being of pure light—a soul who had undergone a transformation so profound that their radiance was blinding. Sarah could feel the energy and wisdom emanating from this being.

The radiant soul spoke with a voice that resonated with the harmony of the universe. "In the Realm of Transformation, we are given the gift of self-discovery and renewal. It is a place where the limitations of the past are shattered, and the infinite potential of the soul is revealed."

Sarah was humbled by the presence of this being, realizing

that her own transformation was just a glimpse of the boundless possibilities that lay before her. She felt a deep sense of gratitude for the opportunity to shed her old self and embrace her true essence.

As she continued to explore the realm, Sarah encountered a mirror, much like the one from the Trial of Self-Reflection, but with a profound difference. This mirror did not just reflect her current self but also showed glimpses of her potential future selves, each one representing a different path and destiny.

She saw herself as an artist, creating masterpieces that inspired and uplifted others. She saw herself as a healer, bringing comfort and healing to those in need. She saw herself as a mentor, guiding others on their journeys of self-discovery. And she saw herself as a seeker of wisdom, delving into the mysteries of existence.

Elias watched as Sarah contemplated the reflections in the mirror. "The Realm of Transformation offers you the opportunity to explore the infinite possibilities of your soul, Sarah. It is a reminder that your journey is not limited by the choices of the past but shaped by the choices of the present and the potential of the future."

Sarah nodded, feeling a sense of empowerment and purpose. She understood that her journey in the afterlife was not just about reflection and healing but also about embracing her true essence and potential. The Realm of Transformation had revealed the depths of her soul and the boundless horizons of her existence.

And so, as she left the realm behind, Sarah carried with her a renewed sense of purpose and a profound understanding of her own potential for growth and transformation. She knew that her journey was far from over, and that the afterlife held even greater revelations and challenges in store.

As Sarah left the Realm of Transformation behind, she felt a profound sense of renewal and purpose. The experiences she had encountered there had reshaped her understanding of her true self and her potential for growth. She knew that her journey in the afterlife was far from over, and that there were still mysteries and revelations to explore.

Guided by Elias, her trusted mentor, she embarked on a new path—one that would take her deeper into the heart of the afterlife and the essence of her own existence.

They walked through a landscape that seemed to shift and change with every step. Radiant colors danced in the air, and surreal vistas stretched out before them. It was a world of endless wonder and possibility, a place where the boundaries of reality and imagination blurred.

Elias spoke with a sense of anticipation, "We are now entering a realm known as the Heart of the Afterlife. It is a place where the very essence of existence is palpable, where the threads of consciousness intertwine."

Sarah looked around, her senses heightened by the energy of the realm. "What will we find here?"

Elias smiled, his eyes filled with a deep wisdom. "In the Heart of the Afterlife, you will find the answers to the most profound questions of existence. It is a place of revelation and awakening."

As they journeyed deeper into the realm, Sarah felt a

sensation of unity and interconnectedness that transcended anything she had ever experienced. She could sense the presence of other souls, not as separate entities, but as threads in the tapestry of consciousness.

She saw a soul who had once been a great philosopher, their thoughts and insights now part of the collective wisdom of the afterlife. She saw a soul who had once been a healer, their compassion and healing energy radiating throughout the realm. She saw souls who had lived lives of courage, creativity, and love, each contributing to the vibrant tapestry of existence.

Elias guided her to a shimmering pool of light at the center of the realm. It seemed to pulse with a rhythmic energy, like the heartbeat of the afterlife itself. Sarah gazed into the pool, feeling a sense of connection to the very essence of existence.

"The Heart of the Afterlife is a place of profound insight and revelation," Elias explained. "It is here that you can gain a deeper understanding of the nature of consciousness, the interconnectedness of all souls, and the purpose of existence."

Sarah watched as images and symbols began to form in the pool, each one representing a facet of the mysteries of existence. She saw the image of a tree with roots that extended deep into the earth, symbolizing the connection between the physical and spiritual realms. She saw a spiral, representing the eternal cycle of growth and renewal. And she saw a radiant sun, signifying the source of all consciousness and light.

As she gazed into the pool, Sarah felt a profound sense of clarity and understanding wash over her. She realized that the afterlife was not just a destination but a journey of the soul, a continuous exploration of consciousness and evolution.

Elias placed a hand on her shoulder, his presence a source of strength and guidance. "In the Heart of the Afterlife, you can gain insights into your own purpose and the role you play in the grand tapestry of existence. It is a place of awakening, where the deepest truths of the soul are revealed."

Sarah nodded, her heart filled with a sense of purpose and wonder. She understood that her journey in the afterlife was a quest for knowledge, a search for meaning, and a commitment to growth and transformation.

As they continued to explore the Heart of the Afterlife, Sarah encountered other souls who were also seeking answers and revelations. They shared stories of their own journeys, their insights, and the profound moments of awakening they had experienced.

One soul, a poet who had once written words of beauty and inspiration, spoke of the power of creativity and expression in the afterlife. They explained how the act of creation was a reflection of the soul's desire to explore and communicate its deepest truths.

Another soul, a philosopher who had pondered the mysteries of existence in life, engaged Sarah in a deep conversation about the nature of consciousness and the interconnectedness of all souls. They discussed the idea that every soul's journey contributed to the collective evolution of consciousness.

As the hours passed, Sarah felt a sense of unity and purpose that transcended her earthly understanding. She realized that her journey was not just about self-discovery but also about contributing to the greater tapestry of existence. Every insight, every revelation, added to the collective wisdom of the afterlife.

And so, as she left the Heart of the Afterlife behind, Sarah carried with her a renewed sense of purpose and a profound understanding of the interconnectedness of all souls. She knew that her journey was far from over, and that the mysteries of existence continued to beckon.

Chapter 10 The Tapestry of Souls

As Sarah's journey through the afterlife continued, she and Elias ventured into a realm known as the Tapestry of Souls. It was a place where the stories and experiences of all souls were interwoven into a magnificent and ever-changing fabric of existence.

The landscape of the Tapestry of Souls was a breathtaking display of color and light. Vast threads of energy stretched out before them, each one representing the unique journey of a soul. The threads wove together in intricate patterns, creating a living tapestry that pulsed with the energy of countless lives.

Elias spoke with reverence, "This is the Tapestry of Souls, Sarah. It is a reflection of the interconnectedness of all existence. Here, you can witness the stories and experiences of every soul who has ever lived."

Sarah gazed in awe at the swirling threads of energy. It was as if she could see the entire history of humanity and beyond, from the earliest moments of consciousness to the present and beyond. She saw moments of joy and moments of sorrow, moments of love and moments of conflict, all woven into the fabric of existence.

Elias gestured to a particular thread, one that seemed to shimmer with a radiant intensity. "Let us follow this thread, Sarah. It represents the journey of a soul who has had a profound impact on the world."

As they followed the thread, Sarah felt herself drawn into the life and experiences of the soul it represented. She saw a woman who had dedicated her life to social justice and equality, a soul who had fought tirelessly for the rights of the marginalized and oppressed.

She witnessed moments of courage as the soul stood up to injustice, moments of compassion as she reached out to those in need, and moments of determination as she never wavered in her commitment to create a more just and equitable world.

Sarah felt a deep sense of connection to the soul's journey, as if she could feel the emotions and experiences as if they were her own. She understood that the Tapestry of Souls was not just a reflection of individual stories but also a reminder of the collective journey of humanity.

Elias spoke softly, "In the Tapestry of Souls, you can gain insights into the interconnectedness of all existence. Every action, every choice, has a ripple effect that extends far beyond the individual soul. It is a reminder of the profound impact each soul can have on the world."

As they continued to follow the threads of the tapestry, Sarah saw a thread that seemed to shimmer with a golden light. It represented the journey of a soul who had devoted their life to the pursuit of knowledge and wisdom. She watched as the soul delved into the mysteries of the universe, seeking to unlock the secrets of existence.

The soul's journey took them to ancient libraries of wisdom, to conversations with sages and scholars, and to moments of profound insight and revelation. Sarah felt a sense of kinship with the soul's quest for knowledge, a reminder of her own thirst for understanding.

Elias nodded, his eyes filled with understanding. "The Tapestry of Souls is a place of reflection and illumination, Sarah. It allows you to witness the diverse paths and experiences of all souls, and to gain insights into the collective wisdom of existence."

As they explored further, Sarah saw a thread that seemed to vibrate with a powerful energy. It represented the journey of a soul who had dedicated their life to the exploration of creativity and artistry. She watched as the soul expressed their innermost thoughts and emotions through music, painting, and dance.

The soul's creations touched the hearts of those who encountered them, inspiring joy, awe, and a sense of connection. Sarah felt a deep resonance with the soul's expression of creativity, a reminder of her own love for art and self-expression.

Elias spoke with a smile, "In the Tapestry of Souls, you can witness the beauty and diversity of human creativity. It is a celebration of the unique gifts and talents that each soul possesses."

As they continued to explore the tapestry, Sarah felt a sense of wonder and gratitude for the opportunity to witness the stories and experiences of all souls. She realized that the afterlife was not just a place of reflection and self-discovery but also a place of connection and unity.

One day, as they followed a particularly intricate thread, Sarah noticed something remarkable. The threads of the tapestry were not static but were constantly shifting and changing, creating new patterns and connections. It was as if the tapestry itself was a living, breathing entity, evolving and adapting with the collective consciousness of all souls.

Elias nodded in acknowledgment. "The Tapestry of Souls is not a static representation but a reflection of the ongoing evolution of consciousness. It reminds us that existence is a dynamic and ever-changing journey."

As Sarah stood before the mesmerizing tapestry, she felt a sense of peace and purpose wash over her. She understood that her own journey was just one thread in the vast tapestry of existence, a part of the greater whole. She realized that every choice, every action, had the potential to create ripples of change that extended far beyond her own life.

Elias placed a hand on her shoulder, his presence a source of comfort and guidance. "The Tapestry of Souls is a reminder that every soul is interconnected, that the choices and experiences of one soul can impact the collective consciousness of all existence. It is a celebration of the unity and diversity of the human experience."

Sarah nodded, her heart filled with a profound sense of gratitude and understanding. She knew that her journey in the afterlife was not just a personal quest for self-discovery but also a contribution to the greater tapestry of existence. She felt a deep sense of purpose and unity with all souls who had ever lived.

And so, as she and Elias continued to explore the Tapestry

of Souls, Sarah carried with her a renewed sense of connection and purpose. She knew that her journey was far from over, and that the mysteries of existence continued to unfold before her.:

Chapter 11: The Garden of Reflection

As Sarah's journey through the afterlife unfolded, she and Elias ventured into a realm known as the Garden of Reflection. It was a place of serene beauty and contemplation, where souls could find solace, healing, and profound insights into their life's journey.

The Garden of Reflection was a lush oasis of vibrant flora, each plant radiating a gentle, soothing light. The air was filled with a sweet, fragrant scent, and the atmosphere resonated with a sense of tranquility. It was a sanctuary for souls seeking moments of introspection and understanding.

Elias spoke with a soft voice, "This is the Garden of Reflection, Sarah. It is a place where souls can find clarity, heal old wounds, and gain deeper insights into their earthly experiences."

Sarah looked around, her eyes taking in the beauty of the garden. She noticed that each plant seemed to have a unique energy, as if it held the wisdom and experiences of a soul. It was a living garden of stories and memories waiting to be explored.

"What will we find here?" Sarah asked, her curiosity piqued.

Elias smiled, his presence a source of comfort. "In the Garden of Reflection, you can explore the memories and emotions that have shaped your journey. It is a place of healing and self-discovery."

As they strolled along a winding path, they approached a tree with leaves that shimmered like emerald jewels. The tree seemed to beckon Sarah, and as she reached out to touch its leaves, she felt a rush of emotions and memories flood her senses.

She saw moments from her childhood, moments of laughter and play, moments of innocence and wonder. She saw the loving embrace of her parents, the wisdom of her grandparents, and the friendships that had sustained her through the years. The tree whispered to her the importance of cherishing the beauty and simplicity of life.

Tears welled up in Sarah's eyes as she relived these cherished memories. It was as if the tree had unlocked a hidden chamber of her heart, allowing her to reconnect with the pure and joyful moments of her past.

Elias nodded in understanding. "The Garden of Reflection allows you to revisit the memories that have shaped your journey. It is a reminder of the beauty and significance of the experiences that have molded you."

As they continued their journey through the garden, Sarah encountered a pond with crystal-clear waters. As she gazed into the pond, she saw reflections of moments of challenge and adversity from her life. She saw the times when she had faced uncertainty, doubt, and fear.

The reflections in the pond showed her the strength and resilience she had demonstrated in those moments. She realized that even in the face of difficulties, she had found the courage to keep moving forward, to learn and grow from her experiences.

Elias spoke with pride, "The Garden of Reflection also allows you to confront the challenges and trials of your journey. It is a place of healing and transformation, where you can gain insights into your own strength and resilience."

As they ventured deeper into the garden, Sarah came across a meadow filled with a multitude of flowers, each one representing a different emotion and experience from her life. There were flowers of joy, sorrow, love, and forgiveness, each one radiating its unique energy.

Sarah reached out to touch one of the flowers, and she felt an overwhelming surge of emotion. It was a flower of gratitude, a reminder of the countless blessings and moments of grace that had graced her life. She realized that even in the midst of challenges, there had always been reasons to be thankful.

Elias spoke softly, "In the Garden of Reflection, you can explore the full spectrum of emotions that have enriched your journey. It is a place of healing and acceptance, where you can embrace the complexity of your own experiences."

As they wandered further, they arrived at a grove of ancient trees, their gnarled roots reaching deep into the earth. The trees seemed to exude a sense of wisdom and resilience, as if they had witnessed the passage of countless ages.

Sarah touched one of the trees, and suddenly, she felt a connection to the collective wisdom of all souls. She saw the interconnectedness of her own journey with the journeys of others, a reminder that she was never alone in her experiences.

Elias nodded in affirmation. "The Garden of Reflection is a place of unity and connection, Sarah. It allows you to explore the interconnectedness of all existence and gain insights from the collective wisdom of souls."

As they continued to explore the garden, Sarah realized that it was not just a place of reflection but also a place of healing and renewal. Each element of the garden—the tree, the pond, the meadow, and the grove of ancient trees—offered a unique opportunity for self-discovery and growth.

One day, as they sat beneath the shade of a majestic tree, Sarah closed her eyes and allowed herself to be enveloped by the tranquility of the garden. She felt a deep sense of peace and acceptance wash over her, as if the garden itself was whispering words of comfort and reassurance.

Elias spoke softly, "The Garden of Reflection is a place where you can find solace and healing, Sarah. It is here that you can come to terms with the complexities of your earthly journey and find inner peace."

Sarah nodded in gratitude, her heart filled with a sense of serenity she had never known before. She understood that the garden was a sanctuary for the soul, a place where she could release the burdens of the past and embrace the beauty of the present.

As the days passed in the Garden of Reflection, Sarah began to notice subtle changes within herself. She felt a deep sense of inner healing, as if old wounds were being gently tended to and transformed into sources of strength. She realized that the garden was not just a place of introspection but also a place of profound healing and renewal.

One evening, as they sat by a tranquil pond, Elias spoke about the power of forgiveness. "Forgiveness is a key that can unlock the doors to healing, Sarah. It is a gift you can give to others and to yourself. Is there someone you need to forgive?"

Sarah closed her eyes and thought about her earthly life. She recalled moments of hurt and betrayal, moments when she had felt wronged by others. And she realized that holding onto these grievances had only weighed her down.

With a deep breath, she whispered, "I forgive. I release these grievances and choose to let go of the pain they have caused."

As she uttered these words, she felt a profound sense of release and lightness. It was as if a heavy burden had been lifted from her heart, allowing her to breathe freely and deeply.

Elias smiled, his eyes filled with warmth. "Forgiveness is a powerful act of self-liberation, Sarah. It allows you to free yourself from the chains of resentment and anger, and to embrace the peace and healing that forgiveness brings."

With each passing day in the Garden of Reflection, Sarah gained deeper insights into her own journey and the importance of self-compassion. She realized that her earthly life had been a tapestry of experiences, each one contributing to her growth and evolution as a soul.

One morning, as she sat amidst the flowers in the meadow, she felt a sense of gratitude welling up within her. She thought about the people who had touched her life, the moments of joy and love, and the opportunities for growth that had come her way.

With tears of gratitude in her eyes, she whispered, "Thank you for the gift of life. Thank you for the lessons and the love."

The flowers seemed to respond, their petals glowing with

a radiant light. It was as if the garden itself was echoing her sentiments, reminding her of the beauty and significance of her earthly journey.

Elias nodded in affirmation. "Gratitude is a powerful force for transformation, Sarah. It allows you to recognize the blessings in your life and to open your heart to even greater abundance."

As her time in the Garden of Reflection continued, Sarah began to sense a deep connection with all souls who had journeyed through the afterlife. She realized that they were all on a shared quest for understanding, healing, and growth. It was a journey of unity and interconnectedness.

One evening, as they watched the sun set over the garden, Elias spoke about the interconnectedness of all existence. "In the grand tapestry of existence, every soul plays a unique role, and every experience contributes to the collective evolution of consciousness."

Sarah gazed at the setting sun, its golden light casting a warm glow over the garden. She felt a profound sense of unity with all souls who had ever lived, a sense of shared purpose and journey.

She whispered, "We are all connected, aren't we? Our journeys are intertwined, and our experiences shape the tapestry of existence."

Elias smiled, his presence a source of wisdom and guidance. "Yes, Sarah. In the Garden of Reflection, you can gain insights into the interconnectedness of all souls and the beauty of the collective journey."

As the days turned into weeks in the Garden of Reflection,

Sarah knew that her time there was coming to an end. She had gained profound insights into her own journey and the interconnectedness of all existence. She had healed old wounds, embraced forgiveness, and found inner peace.

One morning, as she stood beneath the shade of a tree, Elias spoke with a sense of gentle encouragement. "It is time to continue your journey, Sarah. The afterlife has much more to offer, and your path leads to new horizons of discovery and growth."

Sarah nodded, her heart filled with gratitude for the healing and insights she had gained in the garden. She knew that her journey was far from over, and that the mysteries of existence continued to beckon.

And so, as she left the Garden of Reflection behind, Sarah carried with her a renewed sense of inner peace and a profound understanding of the power of healing, forgiveness, and gratitude. She knew that her journey in the afterlife was a quest for self-discovery and unity with all souls who had ever lived.

Chapter 12: The River of Wisdom

After leaving the Garden of Reflection, Sarah and Elias embarked on a new phase of their journey through the afterlife. They found themselves standing at the edge of a vast and serene river known as the River of Wisdom.

The river's waters shimmered with a soft, iridescent glow, and a gentle breeze rustled the leaves of the surrounding trees. It was a place of serenity and contemplation, where souls could come to gain deeper insights into the mysteries of existence.

Elias spoke with a sense of reverence, "This is the River of Wisdom, Sarah. It is a place where the waters of knowledge flow, carrying with them the collective wisdom of all souls who have ever lived."

Sarah looked out at the tranquil river, her eyes drawn to the gentle ripples on its surface. She felt a deep sense of anticipation, a knowing that this river held profound insights waiting to be discovered.

"What will we find here?" she asked, her voice filled with curiosity.

Elias smiled, his presence a source of comfort. "In the River of Wisdom, you can immerse yourself in the collective knowledge of all existence. It is a place of reflection and enlightenment."

As they approached the river, Sarah noticed that it was not just water but a living flow of energy. She extended her hand to touch the waters, and as her fingertips made contact, she felt a surge of awareness rush through her.

Images and symbols began to form in her mind, each one representing a facet of the river's wisdom. She saw the image of an ancient book, its pages filled with the stories and insights of countless souls. She saw a tree of knowledge, its roots reaching deep into the earth and its branches stretching toward the heavens. And she saw a radiant sun, symbolizing the source of all wisdom and light.

Elias watched as Sarah absorbed the river's energy. "The River of Wisdom is a place of revelation and enlightenment, Sarah. It allows you to gain deeper insights into the nature of existence and the mysteries of consciousness."

As they stepped into the river, Sarah felt a profound sense of connection to the collective wisdom of all souls. It was as if she could hear the whispers of countless voices, each one offering a piece of the puzzle that made up the grand tapestry of existence.

She closed her eyes and allowed herself to be carried by the gentle current of the river. As she surrendered to the flow, she began to experience moments of clarity and understanding that transcended her earthly knowledge.

She saw visions of ancient civilizations, their wisdom and knowledge passed down through the ages. She witnessed the discoveries of scientists and philosophers, their quest for understanding shaping the course of human history. She felt the insights of poets and artists, their creations inspired by the depths of the human soul.

Elias spoke softly, "In the River of Wisdom, you can explore the collective knowledge of humanity and gain insights into the eternal truths that have guided souls throughout time."

As they continued to float along the river, Sarah encountered a particularly vibrant section where the waters seemed to dance with a playful energy. She watched as the river transformed into a kaleidoscope of colors, each hue representing a different branch of knowledge and wisdom.

She saw the color blue, symbolizing the wisdom of the oceans and the mysteries of the deep. She saw the color green, representing the knowledge of the natural world and the interconnectedness of all life. She saw the color gold, signifying the wisdom of the ages and the quest for spiritual enlightenment.

Sarah reached out to touch the colorful waters, and as her fingers made contact, she felt a surge of insight and inspiration. It was as if the river itself was offering her gifts of knowledge and understanding.

Elias nodded in acknowledgment. "The River of Wisdom is a place of inspiration and creativity, Sarah. It allows you to tap into the boundless wellspring of knowledge and insight that exists within the collective consciousness of all souls."

As they journeyed further along the river, Sarah encountered a section where the waters seemed to flow through a dense forest of ancient trees. Each tree bore markings and symbols that represented different cultures and traditions from throughout history.

She saw the symbols of ancient civilizations, their languages and art forms preserved in the annals of time. She saw the symbols of indigenous cultures, their deep connection to the earth and the cycles of nature. She saw the symbols of spiritual traditions, their teachings and practices guiding souls toward enlightenment.

Sarah reached out to trace the symbols on the trees, and as her fingers moved over the rough bark, she felt a profound sense of reverence and understanding. It was as if the wisdom of these ancient cultures was being imparted to her, offering insights into the richness of human history and spirituality.

Elias spoke with a sense of awe, "The River of Wisdom allows you to explore the cultural and spiritual diversity of humanity, Sarah. It is a reminder that the quest for knowledge and enlightenment is a universal and timeless journey."

As they continued to float along the river, Sarah noticed

that the waters began to take on a different quality. They became more transparent, as if she could see through the surface into the depths below.

She gazed down and saw glimpses of the past and future intertwined, moments of history and moments yet to come. It was as if time itself was a river, with its currents flowing in both directions.

Elias explained, "In this part of the River of Wisdom, you can gain insights into the nature of time and the interconnectedness of past, present, and future. It is a place of profound understanding and awareness."

Sarah watched as the images of the past and future continued to unfold before her. She saw moments of great change and transformation, moments of challenge and triumph. She realized that time was not a linear progression but a tapestry of experiences, each one shaping the next.

Elias placed a hand on her shoulder, his presence a source of guidance and support. "The River of Wisdom offers you a glimpse into the eternal nature of existence, Sarah. It is a reminder that the journey of the soul transcends the limitations of time and space."

As they approached the end of their journey along the river, Sarah felt a sense of profound gratitude for the insights and wisdom she had gained. She knew that her journey in the afterlife was a quest for understanding and self-discovery, a journey that continued to unfold before her.

Elias spoke with a smile, "The River of Wisdom has offered you a glimpse into the boundless wellspring of knowledge and insight that exists within the collective consciousness of all souls. It is a reminder that the quest for wisdom and understanding is a never-ending journey."

Sarah nodded in agreement, her heart filled with a sense of wonder and reverence for the river's wisdom. She understood that her journey in the afterlife was far from over, and that the mysteries of existence continued to beckon.

And so, as she and Elias left the River of Wisdom behind, Sarah carried with her a renewed sense of understanding and insight. She knew that her journey was a quest for knowledge and enlightenment, a journey that would lead her to even greater revelations and challenges in the afterlife.

Chapter 13: The Library of Eternity

As Sarah and Elias continued their journey through the afterlife, they found themselves standing before a magnificent structure that stretched toward the heavens—an awe-inspiring library known as the Library of Eternity.

The library's towering spires seemed to touch the very sky, and its grand doors stood wide open, inviting souls to enter. The air around it was charged with an energy that hinted at the vast knowledge and wisdom contained within its walls.

Elias spoke with a sense of reverence, "This is the Library of Eternity, Sarah. It is a place where the accumulated knowledge and wisdom of all souls are preserved. Here, you can explore the boundless depths of understanding."

Sarah looked up at the towering library in awe, her heart filled with anticipation. She had always been a lover of books and knowledge, and the prospect of delving into the collective wisdom of all existence filled her with excitement.

"What will we find here?" she asked, her voice trembling with eagerness.

Elias smiled, his presence a source of reassurance. "In the Library of Eternity, you can embark on a journey through the written and unwritten knowledge of all souls. It is a place of discovery and enlightenment."

As they entered the library, Sarah was greeted by the sight of endless shelves, each one filled with books, scrolls, and manuscripts of all shapes and sizes. The shelves stretched out in every direction, disappearing into the horizon.

Sarah's eyes sparkled with wonder as she reached out to touch one of the books. As her fingers brushed the ancient pages, she felt a rush of energy and insight. It was as if the knowledge contained within the book was being absorbed into her very being.

Elias gestured toward the vast expanse of the library. "The Library of Eternity holds the writings and thoughts of all souls who have ever lived. Here, you can explore the diverse perspectives, ideas, and wisdom that have shaped human and spiritual understanding."

Sarah began her exploration by selecting a book from one of the shelves. It was a volume filled with the writings of a philosopher from a distant age, a soul who had pondered the nature of reality and existence.

As she read the philosopher's words, she felt a profound resonance with their thoughts. It was as if the philosopher's insights were speaking directly to her soul, illuminating the mysteries of the universe in ways she had never imagined.

Elias watched as Sarah delved deeper into the philosopher's

writings. "The Library of Eternity allows you to gain insights from the minds and hearts of all souls, Sarah. It is a place where you can expand your understanding of the cosmos and the nature of consciousness."

As she continued to explore, Sarah encountered books on a wide range of topics. She read about the mysteries of the cosmos, the intricacies of quantum physics, and the nature of time and space. She delved into the writings of poets and artists, whose words and creations touched the depths of the human soul.

She immersed herself in the wisdom of ancient sages and modern thinkers, each one offering a unique perspective on the human experience and the quest for spiritual enlightenment. It was a journey through the rich tapestry of human knowledge and understanding.

One day, as she sat amidst a sea of books, Sarah came across a volume that seemed to glow with a radiant light. It was a book of ancient prophecies and visions, written by a soul who had glimpsed the future of humanity.

As she read the prophecies, Sarah felt a sense of awe and wonder. The visions spoke of a time of awakening and transformation, a time when humanity would come to realize its interconnectedness and its potential for greatness.

Elias nodded in acknowledgment. "The Library of Eternity holds not only the knowledge of the past but also glimpses of the future, Sarah. It is a reminder that the journey of the soul extends beyond the boundaries of time and space."

As Sarah continued to explore the library, she began to notice that the books and scrolls seemed to respond to her thoughts and questions. When she wondered about the nature of consciousness, a book on neuroscience and spirituality appeared before her. When she pondered the mysteries of the afterlife, a scroll containing the writings of souls who had journeyed beyond life and death materialized in her hands.

Elias explained, "The Library of Eternity is a place of interactive learning, Sarah. It responds to the inquiries and curiosities of the soul, offering insights and knowledge tailored to your quest for understanding."

Sarah marveled at the library's ability to provide answers to her deepest questions and to guide her on her journey of self-discovery. She realized that the library was not just a repository of knowledge but a living source of wisdom and enlightenment.

One evening, as she sat in a quiet corner of the library, she began to reflect on her own journey through the afterlife. She thought about the insights and experiences she had gained, the moments of healing and transformation, and the profound sense of unity she had discovered.

With a sense of gratitude in her heart, she whispered a silent prayer of thanks to the universe and all the souls who had guided her on her path.

Elias, who had been silently observing, spoke with a smile, "Your journey in the afterlife is a testament to the power of self-discovery and the quest for wisdom, Sarah. It is a reminder that the soul's journey is a continuous exploration of consciousness and growth."

Sarah nodded in agreement, her heart filled with a deep sense of purpose and wonder. She understood that her journey in the afterlife was not just about gaining knowledge but also about contributing to the collective wisdom of all souls who had ever lived.

As she continued to explore the library, she encountered a section that held books and scrolls filled with stories and experiences from the lives of souls who had journeyed through the afterlife. She read about the challenges they had faced, the insights they had gained, and the moments of profound transformation they had experienced.

Elias explained, "The Library of Eternity also contains the stories and experiences of all souls who have explored the afterlife, Sarah. It is a place where you can connect with the journeys and insights of your fellow travelers."

Sarah felt a sense of kinship with the souls whose stories she encountered. She realized that their experiences mirrored her own journey of self-discovery and growth. It was a reminder that the afterlife was a shared realm, where souls supported and learned from each other.

As the days turned into weeks in the Library of Eternity, Sarah knew that her time there was coming to an end. She had gained profound insights into the nature of existence, the mysteries of consciousness, and the interconnectedness of all souls.

Elias spoke with a sense of gentle encouragement, "It is time to continue your journey, Sarah. The afterlife has more to offer, and your path leads to new horizons of discovery and growth."

Sarah nodded in acknowledgment, her heart filled with gratitude for the knowledge and wisdom she had gained in the library. She knew that her journey was far from over, and that the mysteries of existence continued to beckon.

And so, as she left the Library of Eternity behind, Sarah carried with her a renewed sense of understanding and enlightenment. She knew that her journey in the afterlife was a quest for self-discovery and the continuous exploration of consciousness and knowledge

Chapter 14: The Temple of Reflection

After leaving the Library of Eternity, Sarah and Elias continued their journey through the afterlife, guided by an unending sense of wonder and curiosity. Their path led them to a place of profound significance—the Temple of Reflection.

The Temple stood atop a hill, bathed in a soft, ethereal light that seemed to radiate from within. Its architecture was a testament to the grandeur of the afterlife, with intricate carvings and ornate columns that reached toward the heavens.

Elias spoke with a hushed reverence, "This is the Temple of Reflection, Sarah. It is a place of deep introspection and self-discovery. Here, souls come to confront their innermost truths and gain insights into the essence of their being."

Sarah looked up at the majestic temple, her heart filled with anticipation. She had journeyed through realms of knowledge and wisdom, and now, the prospect of exploring the depths of her own soul was both thrilling and humbling.

"What will we find here?" she asked, her voice filled with a mixture of excitement and trepidation.

Elias smiled, his presence a source of unwavering support. "In the Temple of Reflection, you can delve into the essence of your own soul, confront your deepest fears and desires, and gain a profound understanding of your unique journey."

As they entered the temple, Sarah was greeted by a sense of tranquility that seemed to envelop her like a warm embrace. The interior of the temple was adorned with soft candlelight and intricate mosaics that depicted the phases of the moon, symbolizing the cycles of reflection and transformation.

In the center of the temple stood a luminous pool of water, its surface as still as a mirror. It seemed to beckon Sarah, inviting her to gaze into its depths and explore the mysteries within.

Elias led her to the edge of the pool, his voice a soothing presence. "The pool of reflection is a portal to the innermost chambers of your soul, Sarah. It is a place where you can confront your past, embrace your present, and envision your future."

Sarah peered into the pool and watched as images and memories from her earthly life began to surface. She saw moments of joy and moments of sorrow, moments of love and moments of loss. Each image seemed to dance upon the water's surface, telling the story of her life.

As she continued to gaze into the pool, she saw moments of choice and moments of consequence. She witnessed the impact of her actions on others and the ripple effect of her decisions. It was a journey through the tapestry of her own existence.

Elias spoke softly, "The pool of reflection allows you to revisit the moments and choices that have shaped your journey, Sarah. It is a place of healing and understanding."

With a sense of courage, Sarah began to explore the images and memories that emerged from the pool. She saw moments of growth and moments of challenge, moments of self-discovery and moments of doubt.

She saw the times when she had faced her fears and emerged stronger, and she saw the times when she had faltered and learned valuable lessons. It was a journey through the depths of her own soul, a journey toward self-acceptance and understanding.

Elias watched as Sarah confronted her own truths with courage and grace. "The Temple of Reflection is a place of profound self-discovery, Sarah. It allows you to embrace the complexity of your own experiences and find healing and acceptance."

As Sarah continued to explore the pool of reflection, she noticed that the water's surface began to shift and change, revealing visions of her present and future. She saw glimpses of the afterlife and the limitless possibilities it held.

She saw herself connecting with other souls, sharing wisdom and insights, and contributing to the collective consciousness of all existence. She realized that her journey in the afterlife was not just a personal quest for self-discovery but also a contribution to the greater tapestry of existence.

Elias spoke with a sense of affirmation, "The Temple of Reflection allows you to envision your future and embrace the infinite potential of your soul, Sarah. It is a place of inspiration and transformation."

With newfound clarity and purpose, Sarah felt a deep sense of gratitude for the opportunity to explore the depths of her own soul. She knew that her journey was far from over, and that the mysteries of existence continued to unfold before her.

One day, as she sat in quiet contemplation within the temple, she felt a presence beside her—a presence that emanated a profound sense of love and guidance. She turned to see a luminous figure, radiant with light and grace.

The figure spoke with a voice that resonated with wisdom and compassion. "I am a guardian of the Temple of Reflection, Sarah. I am here to assist you on your journey of self-discovery and transformation."

Sarah felt a deep sense of trust and connection with the guardian. She realized that this encounter was not a mere coincidence but a profound moment of guidance and support.

With a sense of humility, she asked, "What wisdom do you have to share with me?"

The guardian smiled, their presence filling the temple with a gentle radiance. "In the depths of your soul, Sarah, you hold the key to your own transformation. Embrace your past with gratitude, your present with awareness, and your future with boundless potential."

As Sarah absorbed the guardian's words, she felt a profound sense of empowerment and clarity. She understood that her journey in the afterlife was a journey toward self-acceptance, growth, and the realization of her true potential.

Elias nodded in affirmation, his presence a source of encouragement. "The Temple of Reflection is a place of empowerment, Sarah. It allows you to confront your own truths and envision the path of your soul's evolution."

With a renewed sense of purpose, Sarah continued her exploration of the Temple of Reflection. She found herself drawn to a series of ornate doors that seemed to radiate a sense of mystery and promise. As she approached them, she realized that each door led to a chamber of the temple, each one representing a different aspect of her soul's journey.

The first door she entered led to a chamber filled with mirrors of various shapes and sizes. Each mirror reflected a different aspect of herself—the joyful, the wounded, the courageous, the curious. Sarah gazed into each mirror, seeing the facets of her own soul with compassion and acceptance. She realized that self-love and self-acceptance were key to her inner transformation.

The second door opened into a chamber adorned with paintings and murals that depicted pivotal moments from her earthly life. She saw moments of challenge and moments of triumph, moments of connection and moments of solitude. It was a visual narrative of her journey, and as she studied each painting, she gained a deeper understanding of the lessons and blessings of her life.

The third door led to a chamber filled with the soothing sound of flowing water. In the center of the chamber was a tranquil pool, much like the one at the entrance of the temple. But this pool was special—it held reflections of her dreams and aspirations. Sarah gazed into the pool, seeing images of her future self, of the person she aspired to become. It was a reminder that her journey was a continuous evolution toward her highest potential.

The fourth door revealed a chamber illuminated by a soft,

radiant light. In the center of the room was a luminous crystal that seemed to pulse with energy. Sarah approached the crystal and placed her hand upon it. She felt a surge of insight and intuition flow through her. It was a chamber of intuition and inner guidance, a reminder that her inner wisdom was a powerful compass on her journey.

Elias watched as Sarah explored the chambers of the temple with a sense of curiosity and self-discovery. "The Temple of Reflection allows you to explore the multi-dimensional aspects of your own soul, Sarah. It is a place where you can integrate your past, embrace your present, and envision your future."

As Sarah continued her journey through the temple, she encountered a series of passages and corridors that seemed to lead deeper into the heart of her own consciousness. Each passage held its own challenges and revelations, testing her resolve and pushing her to confront her own truths.

In one passage, she faced a shadowy figure that seemed to embody her deepest fears and insecurities. The figure taunted her with doubts and uncertainties, but Sarah, fortified by her journey of self-reflection, found the inner strength to confront and dispel these shadows.

In another passage, she encountered a series of mirrors that reflected her own judgments and self-criticism. She realized that these judgments were barriers to her own growth and self-acceptance. With courage and self-compassion, she shattered the mirrors, liberating herself from self-imposed limitations.

In yet another passage, she found herself in a chamber

filled with the sound of her own inner voice—the voice that had guided her through moments of doubt and confusion, the voice of intuition and wisdom. She listened to her inner guidance, trusting that it would lead her toward her highest potential.

Elias spoke with pride, "The Temple of Reflection challenges you to confront your own limitations and fears, Sarah. It is a place of empowerment and transformation, where you can emerge stronger and more self-aware."

As Sarah emerged from the deepest chambers of the temple, she felt a profound sense of transformation and renewal. She had confronted her own truths, embraced her past with gratitude, and envisioned her future with boundless potential. She understood that her journey in the afterlife was a continuous evolution of consciousness and self-discovery.

One evening, as she sat in quiet contemplation within the temple, she felt a presence beside her—a presence that emanated a profound sense of peace and fulfillment. It was the guardian of the temple, their luminous form radiating a sense of completeness.

The guardian spoke with a voice that resonated with wisdom and love. "You have journeyed deep within the chambers of your own soul, Sarah. You have confronted your own truths and embraced your own potential. It is time to carry this wisdom and transformation forward on your journey."

Sarah nodded in gratitude, her heart filled with a deep sense of fulfillment. She knew that her journey in the afterlife was a testament to the power of self-discovery and the continuous exploration of consciousness.

With a sense of purpose and self-acceptance, she left the Temple of Reflection behind, carrying with her a renewed understanding of her own soul and the infinite possibilities that lay before her.

And so, as Sarah and Elias continued their journey through the afterlife, they knew that the mysteries of existence continued to beckon. The temple had been a place of profound self-discovery and transformation, a reminder that the soul's journey was a continuous exploration of consciousness and growth.

Chapter 15: The Realm of Dreams

After leaving the Temple of Reflection, Sarah and Elias embarked on a new phase of their journey through the afterlife. Their path led them to a realm of enchantment and mystery—the Realm of Dreams.

This realm seemed to stretch endlessly in all directions, with ethereal landscapes that shifted and transformed like the contents of a dream. Colors swirled and blended in mesmerizing patterns, and the air was filled with a gentle, melodic hum that seemed to resonate with the very essence of existence.

Elias spoke with a sense of wonder, "Welcome to the Realm of Dreams, Sarah. This is a place where the boundaries of reality and imagination are blurred, where the dreams of souls take shape and come to life."

Sarah looked around in awe, her senses overwhelmed by the beauty and fluidity of this realm. She had entered a world where dreams and imagination held sway, and the possibilities seemed limitless.

"What will we find here?" she asked, her voice filled with curiosity.

Elias smiled, his presence a source of guidance and reassurance. "In the Realm of Dreams, you can explore the dreams and aspirations of all souls, gain insights into the power of creativity and imagination, and experience the boundless potential of consciousness."

As they ventured deeper into the realm, Sarah realized that the landscapes and scenery were shaped by the thoughts and desires of the souls who passed through. She watched as trees sprouted from the ground, their leaves forming intricate patterns of color. She saw rivers that flowed with liquid light, and mountains that shimmered like precious gems.

Elias explained, "In the Realm of Dreams, the very fabric of reality is shaped by the collective dreams and intentions of all souls. It is a reminder of the creative power that resides within each soul."

Sarah marveled at the idea that the landscape around her was a reflection of the dreams and intentions of all souls who had ever lived. It was a testament to the interconnectedness of all existence, where individual dreams merged into a tapestry of collective creation.

As they continued to explore, Sarah noticed that the realm was filled with beings of light and energy, each one embodying a different dream or aspiration. She saw beings of joy and laughter, beings of healing and compassion, and beings of inspiration and innovation.

She approached one of these beings, a radiant figure whose

presence exuded a sense of serenity and contentment. "What is your dream?" she asked.

The being smiled, its energy dancing with light. "My dream is to bring peace and harmony to all souls, to help them find the serenity within their own hearts."

Sarah felt a sense of resonance with the being's dream. She realized that the realm was not just a place of dreams but also a place of connection, where souls could share their dreams and aspirations, and find support and inspiration from one another.

Elias nodded in affirmation, "In the Realm of Dreams, you can connect with the dreams and intentions of all souls, Sarah. It is a place of unity and shared vision."

As they journeyed further into the realm, Sarah began to notice that she could shape the environment with her own thoughts and intentions. She experimented with her creative power, and to her amazement, she saw flowers bloom at her command, and stars form constellations in the sky.

Elias encouraged her exploration, "The Realm of Dreams is a place where your own creative potential is magnified, Sarah. It is a reminder that the power of imagination and intention can shape your reality."

With newfound understanding, Sarah realized that she could use her creative abilities to not only shape the landscape but also to explore her own dreams and aspirations. She closed her eyes and allowed her thoughts to drift into the realm of possibility.

She saw herself surrounded by books, each one filled with stories and wisdom. It was a dream of knowledge and learning, a reflection of her passion for understanding the mysteries of existence.

She saw herself standing on a stage, speaking to a vast audience. It was a dream of sharing wisdom and inspiration, a reflection of her desire to uplift and empower others.

She saw herself in a peaceful garden, surrounded by flowers and flowing water. It was a dream of serenity and healing, a reflection of her longing for inner peace and harmony.

Elias watched as Sarah's dreams and aspirations took shape in the realm, her thoughts and intentions manifesting into vibrant scenes and experiences. "The Realm of Dreams is a place where your dreams and aspirations come to life, Sarah. It is a reminder that your thoughts and intentions hold the power to shape your reality."

As Sarah continued to explore her dreams and aspirations in the realm, she encountered a series of portals that seemed to lead to different aspects of her own consciousness. Each portal held the promise of self-discovery and transformation.

The first portal led to a chamber filled with mirrors that reflected her past experiences and choices. She saw moments of joy and moments of challenge, moments of growth and moments of introspection. It was a journey through the tapestry of her own life, a reflection of the choices that had brought her to this moment.

The second portal revealed a chamber adorned with paintings and murals that depicted her present experiences and relationships. She saw herself surrounded by friends and loved ones, each one playing a unique role in her journey. It was a visual narrative of her current existence, a reflection of the connections that enriched her life.

The third portal opened into a chamber filled with the soothing sound of flowing water. In the center of the chamber was a tranquil pool, much like the one at the entrance of the temple. But this pool was special—it held reflections of her future dreams and aspirations. Sarah gazed into the pool, seeing images of her own potential and the path that lay before her. It was a reminder that her journey was a continuous evolution toward her highest self.

The fourth portal revealed a chamber illuminated by a soft, radiant light. In the center of the room was a luminous crystal that seemed to pulse with energy. Sarah approached the crystal and placed her hand upon it. She felt a surge of insight and intuition flow through her. It was a chamber of inner wisdom and guidance, a reminder that her inner voice was a powerful compass on her journey.

Elias watched as Sarah explored the chambers of self-discovery and transformation with a sense of courage and introspection. "The Realm of Dreams challenges you to explore the multi-dimensional aspects of your own consciousness, Sarah. It is a place of empowerment and self-awareness."

Chapter 16: The Path of Integration

After their profound experiences in the Realm of Dreams, Sarah and Elias embarked on the next leg of their journey through the afterlife. Their path led them to a place known as the Path of Integration.

This path was unlike any they had encountered before. It stretched out before them, weaving through a landscape of ever-changing colors and forms. It was as if they were walking through the very fabric of existence, where all aspects of consciousness converged and merged.

Elias spoke with a sense of reverence, "Welcome to the Path of Integration, Sarah. This is a place where the fragmented aspects of the self come together, where the threads of experience and knowledge unite to form a greater whole."

Sarah looked around in wonder, trying to make sense of the swirling colors and forms that surrounded her. It was as if she had entered a realm where past, present, and future existed simultaneously, where all the experiences and knowledge she had gained in her journey converged.

"What will we find here?" she asked, her voice filled with curiosity.

Elias smiled, his presence a source of guidance and support. "In the Path of Integration, you can merge your past, present, and future experiences into a harmonious whole. It is a place of self-discovery and synthesis."

As they ventured deeper into the path, Sarah began to notice that the colors and forms around her represented different aspects of her own consciousness. She saw vibrant hues of joy and laughter, swirling patterns of curiosity and wonder, and deep, tranquil pools of introspection and contemplation.

Elias explained, "In the Path of Integration, the fragmented aspects of the self are brought together into a unified whole, Sarah. It is a reminder that your journey is not just a series of separate experiences but a tapestry of interconnected wisdom."

Sarah marveled at the idea that all her experiences and

knowledge were interwoven into a greater tapestry of understanding. It was a testament to the richness of her journey and the interconnectedness of all existence.

As they continued to walk along the path, Sarah began to feel a sense of resonance with the different aspects of her consciousness. She noticed that her thoughts and emotions began to merge and harmonize, creating a sense of inner peace and unity.

Elias watched with pride as Sarah began to integrate the fragmented aspects of her own consciousness. "The Path of Integration allows you to harmonize your inner experiences and knowledge, Sarah. It is a place of inner balance and synthesis."

With newfound clarity and self-awareness, Sarah realized that the path also offered her the opportunity to integrate her past, present, and future experiences. She closed her eyes and allowed her thoughts to drift into the realm of possibility.

She saw herself as a child, full of innocence and curiosity, exploring the wonders of the world with wide-eyed wonder. She felt a sense of connection to her younger self, recognizing that the essence of who she was had always been a part of her.

She saw herself in the present moment, navigating the complexities of life with grace and resilience. She felt a deep sense of acceptance for her current self, recognizing that every choice and experience had led her to this point.

She saw herself in the future, standing on the threshold of new adventures and possibilities. She felt a sense of anticipation and excitement for the person she was becoming, recognizing that the future was a canvas waiting to be painted.

Elias spoke with a sense of affirmation, "The Path of Integration allows you to merge your past, present, and future into a seamless tapestry of experience, Sarah. It is a reminder that your journey is a continuous evolution of consciousness."

As they journeyed further along the path, Sarah encountered a series of portals that seemed to lead to different aspects of her own consciousness. Each portal held the promise of self-discovery and transformation.

The first portal led to a chamber filled with mirrors that reflected her past experiences and choices. She saw moments of joy and moments of challenge, moments of growth and moments of introspection. It was a journey through the tapestry of her own life, a reflection of the choices that had brought her to this moment.

The second portal revealed a chamber adorned with paintings and murals that depicted her present experiences and relationships. She saw herself surrounded by friends and loved ones, each one playing a unique role in her journey. It was a visual narrative of her current existence, a reflection of the connections that enriched her life.

The third portal opened into a chamber filled with the soothing sound of flowing water. In the center of the chamber was a tranquil pool, much like the one at the entrance of the temple. But this pool was special—it held reflections of her future dreams and aspirations. Sarah gazed into the pool, seeing images of her own potential and the path that lay before her. It was a reminder that her journey was a continuous evolution toward her highest self.

The fourth portal revealed a chamber illuminated by a

soft, radiant light. In the center of the room was a luminous crystal that seemed to pulse with energy. Sarah approached the crystal and placed her hand upon it. She felt a surge of insight and intuition flow through her. It was a chamber of inner wisdom and guidance, a reminder that her inner voice was a powerful compass on her journey.

Elias watched as Sarah explored the chambers of self-discovery and transformation with a sense of courage and introspection. "The Path of Integration challenges you to harmonize your inner experiences and knowledge, Sarah. It is a place of empowerment and self-awareness."

As Sarah emerged from the deepest chambers of the path, she felt a profound sense of transformation and renewal. She had integrated the fragmented aspects of her own consciousness, harmonizing her past, present, and future experiences into a seamless tapestry of understanding. She understood that her journey in the afterlife was a continuous evolution of consciousness and self-discovery.

One evening, as she sat in quiet contemplation along the path, she felt a presence beside her—a presence that emanated a profound sense of unity and completeness. It was the guardian of the path, their luminous form radiating a sense of fulfillment.

The guardian spoke with a voice that resonated with wisdom and love. "You have journeyed deep within the chambers of your own consciousness, Sarah. You have integrated the fragmented aspects of your self and embraced the unity of your experiences. It is time to carry this wisdom and transformation forward on your journey."

Sarah nodded in gratitude, her heart filled with a deep sense of fulfillment. She knew that her journey in the afterlife was a testament to the power of self-discovery and the continuous exploration of consciousness.

With a sense of purpose and unity, she left the Path of Integration behind, carrying with her a renewed understanding of her own consciousness and the interconnectedness of all existence.

And so, as Sarah and Elias continued their journey through the afterlife, they knew that the mysteries of existence continued to beckon. The path had been a place of profound self-discovery and transformation, a reminder that the soul's journey was a continuous evolution of consciousness and growth.

Chapter 17: The Symphony of Souls

As Sarah and Elias continued their journey through the afterlife, they found themselves in a realm that resonated with a profound sense of harmony and unity—the Symphony of Souls.

This realm was unlike any they had encountered before. It was a vast expanse of vibrant energy and light, where every soul that had ever existed was represented as a unique musical note. These notes blended together in a harmonious symphony that filled the air with a melodious and transcendent sound.

Elias spoke with a sense of awe, "Welcome to the Symphony of Souls, Sarah. This is a place where the collective consciousness of all existence is expressed as a symphony of harmony and unity."

Sarah stood still, her senses overwhelmed by the beauty and serenity of the symphony. It was as if the very essence of existence was resonating in perfect harmony, creating a tapestry of interconnectedness.

"What is this place?" she asked in hushed wonder.

Elias smiled, his presence a source of reassurance and guidance. "In the Symphony of Souls, you can experience the interconnectedness of all existence, gain insights into the collective wisdom of souls, and join in the creation of a harmonious whole."

As they ventured deeper into the realm, Sarah realized that the notes of the symphony were not just abstract sounds but representations of individual souls. Each note carried a unique frequency and vibration, and together, they created a symphony that transcended time and space.

She noticed that the symphony was not just a passive creation but an active and evolving expression of the souls that composed it. Souls flowed through the symphony, merging and harmonizing their energies in an ever-changing dance of unity.

Elias explained, "In the Symphony of Souls, you can connect with the energies and intentions of all souls, Sarah. It is a place of unity and shared expression."

As they continued to explore, Sarah felt a sense of resonance with the symphony. She realized that her own energy and essence were a part of this harmonious whole, contributing to the collective tapestry of existence.

She extended her senses further and began to hear the melodies of individual souls. She heard the notes of joy and laughter, the notes of sorrow and healing, and the notes of wisdom and inspiration. It was as if the souls were speaking to her through their unique frequencies.

Elias watched with a sense of pride as Sarah began to attune herself to the symphony. "The Symphony of Souls allows you to listen to the voices and intentions of all souls, Sarah. It is a place of deep connection and shared wisdom."

With newfound understanding, Sarah realized that the symphony also offered her the opportunity to contribute her own unique note to the collective harmony. She closed her eyes and allowed her own energy and intention to flow into the symphony.

She felt her note merge with the others, creating a beautiful and harmonious chord that resonated with love and unity. It was a reminder that her presence in the afterlife was not just about receiving but also about giving, about contributing to the greater symphony of existence.

Elias spoke with a sense of affirmation, "The Symphony of Souls allows you to express your own unique energy and intention, Sarah. It is a place of co-creation and shared expression."

As they journeyed further into the realm, Sarah realized that the symphony also had the power to reflect the experiences and intentions of all souls. She noticed that the melodies of the symphony shifted and changed, responding to the thoughts and emotions of the souls that composed it.

She witnessed moments of joy and celebration, where the symphony soared with exuberant melodies. She witnessed moments of introspection and contemplation, where the symphony took on a serene and meditative quality. It was a reflection of the collective consciousness and the ever-changing nature of existence.

Elias explained, "The Symphony of Souls is a mirror of the experiences and intentions of all souls, Sarah. It is a reminder that your thoughts and emotions have the power to shape your reality."

With this realization, Sarah became more attuned to her own thoughts and intentions, understanding that they had a direct impact on the symphony and the collective consciousness. She began to channel her intentions toward love, harmony, and unity, knowing that her energy contributed to the greater whole.

As they continued to explore, Sarah noticed that the symphony had a transformative power. It had the ability to heal and uplift the souls that experienced it. She witnessed souls who had carried burdens of sorrow and pain being enveloped by the healing melodies of the symphony, their energies transforming into states of peace and serenity.

Elias watched with a sense of compassion as Sarah witnessed these moments of transformation. "The Symphony of Souls has the power to heal and uplift, Sarah. It is a place of profound healing and transformation."

With a sense of purpose, Sarah began to channel her intentions toward healing and transformation, extending her energy to those souls who sought solace and renewal in the symphony. She felt a deep sense of connection and compassion for all the souls she encountered.

One evening, as she sat in quiet contemplation within

the symphony, she felt a presence beside her—a presence that emanated a profound sense of love and guidance. She turned to see a luminous figure,

Chapter 18: The Heart of Understanding

The luminous figure who had appeared beside Sarah in the Symphony of Souls radiated a warm and comforting presence. It was as if a gentle light enveloped them, illuminating the space around them.

The figure spoke with a voice that resonated with wisdom and love. "I am a guardian of the Symphony of Souls, Sarah. I am here to assist you on your journey of connection and understanding."

Sarah felt an immediate sense of trust and connection with the guardian. She knew that this encounter was not a mere coincidence but a profound moment of guidance and support.

With a sense of humility, she asked, "What wisdom do you have to share with me?"

The guardian smiled, their presence filling the symphony with a deep sense of peace. "In the Symphony of Souls, you have witnessed the interconnectedness of all existence, the power of shared intention, and the transformative nature of harmony. It is a reflection of the unity that underlies all creation."

Sarah nodded, her heart filled with a sense of understanding. She had experienced the symphony as a place of connection and unity, a reminder that all souls were part of a greater whole.

The guardian continued, "But there is a deeper layer of

understanding that the symphony can offer, Sarah. It is the understanding of the heart, the recognition that love is the essence of all existence."

Sarah listened intently, her curiosity piqued. She had journeyed through realms of knowledge and wisdom, and now she was ready to explore the profound wisdom of the heart.

The guardian spoke with a gentle assurance, "The heart is the seat of love and compassion, the source of empathy and understanding. In the Symphony of Souls, you have the opportunity to connect with the heart of all souls, to experience the depth of love that unites all existence."

With the guardian as her guide, Sarah closed her eyes and allowed her awareness to shift from the melodies of the symphony to the heartbeats of the souls that composed it. She felt a subtle shift in her perception, as if she was attuning herself to the very essence of existence.

She heard the heartbeats of souls pulsating with love and compassion, each one like a radiant star in the symphony. She heard the heartbeats of souls seeking healing and understanding, their energies calling out for love and solace.

Elias watched with a sense of pride as Sarah connected with the heartbeats of the souls in the symphony. "The heart is the gateway to understanding and compassion, Sarah. It is a place of profound connection and empathy."

As she continued to attune herself to the heartbeats, Sarah noticed that each heartbeat carried a unique signature, a resonance that was as individual as the soul it represented. Yet, beneath this individuality, there was a common thread of love that united them all.

The guardian spoke softly, "In the heart of understanding, you can connect with the essence of love that unites all souls, Sarah. It is a reminder that love is the universal language of the soul."

Sarah felt a deep sense of gratitude for the opportunity to connect with the heartbeats of the souls in the symphony. It was a profound experience of unity and empathy, a recognition that love was the unifying force that transcended all differences.

With the guardian's guidance, she extended her own heart energy to the souls in the symphony, offering love and compassion to those who sought healing and understanding. She felt her own heart expand with each act of love, knowing that her intentions were contributing to the greater harmony of the symphony.

Elias spoke with a sense of affirmation, "The heart of understanding allows you to express your own love and compassion, Sarah. It is a place of shared empathy and healing."

As they continued to explore the heart of understanding, Sarah realized that it also held the power to heal and transform her own consciousness. She felt her own heart energy being uplifted and purified, as if the very act of giving love and compassion was a source of inner renewal.

The guardian explained, "In the heart of understanding, you not only connect with the essence of love in all souls but also experience the healing and transformation of your own heart, Sarah. It is a place of deep inner renewal."

With this realization, Sarah allowed her own heart to be transformed by the love and compassion she extended to others. She felt a deep sense of inner peace and fulfillment, a recognition that love was the key to her own evolution of consciousness.

One evening, as she sat in quiet contemplation within the heart of understanding, she felt a presence beside her—a presence that emanated a profound sense of love and unity. She turned to see the luminous figure, the guardian of the Symphony of Souls, standing beside her.

The guardian spoke with a voice filled with love and wisdom. "You have journeyed to the heart of understanding, Sarah, and in doing so, you have experienced the depth of love that unites all souls. It is a reminder that love is the essence of all existence."

Sarah nodded, her heart filled with a sense of profound understanding and connection. She knew that her journey in the afterlife was not just about acquiring knowledge and wisdom but also about experiencing the transformative power of love.

The guardian continued, "As you carry this wisdom of the heart with you, remember that love is the universal language of the soul, the bridge that unites all differences. It is a reminder that every soul, no matter how unique, is connected by the thread of love."

With a sense of gratitude and love, Sarah left the Symphony of Souls behind, carrying with her the wisdom of the heart and the recognition that love was the essence of all existence.

And so, as Sarah and Elias continued their journey through the afterlife, they knew that the mysteries of existence continued to beckon. The heart of understanding had been a place of profound connection and compassion, a reminder that love was the universal language of the soul.